INDIAN AND WESTERN PHILOSOPHY

A Study in Contrasts

INDIAN AND WESTERN PHILOSOPHY

A Study in Contrasts

BY

BETTY HEIMANN, Ph.D.

Late Professor in the University of Halle-Wittenberg,
Lecturer in Sanskrit and Indian Philosophy
in the School of Oriental Studies,
University of London

LONDON
GEORGE ALLEN & UNWIN LTD
MUSEUM STREET

FIRST PUBLISHED IN 1937

PRINTED IN GREAT BRITAIN BY
UNWIN BROTHERS LTD., WOKING

THE MOTTO OF THE WEST:

Πάντων χρημάτων μέτρον ἄνθρωπος.

Man is the Measure of all things.

(Protagoras, *c.* 500 B.C.)

THE MOTTO OF INDIA:

eṣa ātmā samaḥ pluṣiṇā samo maśakena samo nāgena sama ebhis tribhir lokaiḥ . . . samo 'nena sarveṇa.

This Ātman (the vital essence in Man) is the same in the ant, the same in the gnat, the same in the elephant, the same in these three worlds, . . . the same in the whole universe.

(*Bṛhadaranyaka-upaniṣad* 1, 3, 22, *c.* 1000 B.C.)

PREFACE

This comparative study of Indian and Western philosophical ideas is based on the Forlong Fund Lectures, under the auspices of the Royal Asiatic Society, which I was invited to deliver in the Lent Term, 1936, as a special course at the School of Oriental Studies, University of London.

I wish to express my gratitude to the Forlong Fund Committee for having given me the opportunity to present my subject to an English audience.

BETTY HEIMANN

LONDON

June 1937

CONTENTS

INDIAN AND WESTERN PHILOSOPHY

CHAPTER I

INTRODUCTION

Une œuvre d'art est un coin de la création vu à travers un tempérament, says Zola; and we may be justified in applying this aphorism when we venture on a somewhat similar survey and attempt an artificial selection from World-Philosophy throughout the ages. My aim, however, is not to elaborate any finished outline of all the philosophical conceptions that have arisen in East and West up to the present day, but merely to indicate the essential and fundamental tendencies and principles.

In tracing the sources of Western Philosophy to Plato and Aristotle, and still earlier to the pre-Socratics of ancient Greece, I became convinced that all translations are, to a greater or less degree, modes of interpretation. I studied the Classics, therefore, from the linguistic standpoint, and this procedure ultimately developed into a philosophical method intimately associated with the psychological aspects of Philology. In pursuing this task I discovered at the same time the specifically material basis of all

Western thought. In other words—in my regress from the history of modern Philosophy to the dawn of Greek speculation, or (to repeat) to the pre-Socratics, I found myself able to trace the main trends of Western Philosophy to the prior era of the Greek Sophists, whose outstanding rôle as the actual founders of Western thought is, in my opinion, too frequently underestimated. Their basic dogma—which has held good in the West ever since—was, "Man is the Measure of all things": *πάντων χρημάτων μέτρον ἄνθρωπος.*

At this point an equally important feature must be emphasized; for throughout this age of the Sophists there persists the profound contrast between the typically Western, and the equally distinctive Eastern, intellectual and spiritual atmospheres. In this connection, still further, I was deeply impressed by the far-reaching divergence of the Western anthropological tendency from the older cosmic outlook upon Man as "being part and parcel of the Universe." And this radical antithesis is to be discerned in contemporary Greek drama. For Aeschylus, the *Marathonomaches*, creates all his immortal tragedies in the genuinely cosmic mood. Every infraction of cosmic order, with no single exception, must generate its own inevitable reaction, and also its punishment, in order that the primal cosmic harmony may once more be restored. Hence it is that in Aeschylean drama the curse invoked on the offender extends to his descendants; hence, too,

Aeschylus' vehement condemnation of human *hybris* —of human vanity and self-righteousness.

Sophocles again, the eclectic poet and thinker, whose early tragedies were composed under the influence of the ancient law of the same Aeschylean type, realizes in his first *Oedipus, Oedipus Basileus*, the radical perversion of cosmic order which Oedipus himself has caused. To him it makes not the slightest difference whether Oedipus consciously, or unconsciously, commits the unspeakable crime of killing his own father and marrying his mother; it is, rather, precisely the unnaturalness of these deeds that must be atoned for. Cosmic law has been violated: its integrity, therefore, must be restored by the sinner's dire punishment. Later still Sophocles, but again as the eclectic, was deeply influenced by the new anthropological principle enunciated by the Sophist Antiphon; and now he deals with intent (*dolos*), the doer's own personal attitude towards the crime. It is then in accordance with this radically changed viewpoint that Sophocles is inspired to write a second *Oedipus, Oedipus in Kolonos*, in which he regards Oedipus' guilt from the new Sophistic angle: "Man is the measure of all things." From this standpoint the second Oedipus justly denies his guilt, for he has not acted consciously; in the light of the freshly recognized standards of human measure, consciousness and intent, therefore, he is perfectly innocent. It is most illuminating to compare Sophocles' two *Oedipus* dramas with regard to their fundamentally divergent outlook and profoundly different argument.

Having thus detected the starting-point of an anthropological, as distinguished from a cosmic, canon in the West, I passed on to the study of the pre-Sophistic, or cosmic, thinkers of ancient Greece; but feeling dissatisfied with tracing their speculations merely during the relatively brief period of early Greek Philosophy, comprising Thales (*c.* 650 B.C.) and the Sophists (*c.* 500 B.C.), I searched for an opportunity to consider these typical cosmic ideas in still further detail and through a yet longer period.

Now there is only one region where such cosmic principles could develop under the most favourable possible conditions, and completely undisturbed from without, until they became finally consolidated and firmly established—that is in India.

For this vast and almost isolated triangular continent is separated from the outer world by perilous seas and high mountain ranges with few practicable passes, thus permitting only a relatively limited mass of invaders to enter at any given time. Every influx of newcomers, therefore, was almost wholly absorbed by the indigenes before another could follow. India, consequently, has a history all her own. I have myself seen a caravan toiling along the Khyber Pass at an incredibly slow pace, and I was deeply impressed by discovering that this ancient road still continues to be the main route for traffic between the remote countries of Inner Asia and the fertile plains of Northern India. Thus both climatically and geographically India was predestined for the full development of cosmic speculation. Here Nature still remains the *force majeure* in spite of steadily encroaching Western technics; and as contrasted with India's powerful and rapacious animals and prolific vegetation, Man can enjoy no outstanding predominance. India, then, has based all her fundamental concepts, in both science and art alike, on the dominating presupposition of the *force majeure* of an almost eternal and irresistible tropical Nature. Here therefore Man was, and ever remained, no more than part and parcel of the mighty Whole.

Thus I became an Indologist, more than ever convinced of the necessity for associating together Philology and Philosophy;[1] for these unique geographical and historical conditions of India must serve to account for her characteristically ambiguous linguistic forms of expression. Thus every student of the ancient Indian *Texts* is compelled to be a synthetic thinker, while only the philologically trained interpreter will be in any proper position to grasp the manifold diversity of both the underlying rational meanings and the irrational interconnections of almost every Indian term without exception.[2]

Still, we must ask, why should an Indologist, with some interest in general philosophical problems, undertake the supremely difficult task of a comparative study of the Philosophy of East and West?

[1] *Cf.* my article "Psychology of Indian Grammar," *Archiv Orientalny*, 1935.

[2] *Cf.* Index, pp. 148 ff.

My justification is that India offers to our Western world a unique opportunity of learning by means of striking contrasts. For in India the distinctly cosmic outlook has been thoroughly developed in all its logical consequences, while at the same time it is being constantly renewed by the prevailing natural conditions. India's unchanging, and indeed almost unchangeable, world forms the completest possible antithesis to the West, subject as it is to the incessant vicissitudes caused by historical and technical necessitities.

In the Western temperate zone and its vast and open areas, then, Man may, and indeed must, radically modify the course of Nature; not so, however, in the tropical heart of Indian culture. It was therefore inevitable that at even so early a period as the pre-Christian days of the Greek Sophists, the West should discover the fact that the conditions of our temperate zone can and must be dominated by Man's skill and intellectual capacities.

Thus by comparing these two differently based groups of cultures which, while quite consistent in themselves, have at the same time been closely adapted to their specific natural conditions, we are enabled to perceive more clearly the outlines of our own Western culture, and to extend our ken far beyond the narrow limits set by our own orientation; and so we realize that the line of development followed in the West is by no means the only possible one for all climates. This comparative method yields different results, springing from markedly different fundamental principles—Western Anthropology on the one hand and Indian Cosmology on the other; Western expansion of Philosophy as a steady progress, yet with an ever-changing outlook, and Indian development as a radiation, an emanation, from a few basic ideas maintained for at least four thousand years. Our comparison, still further, may serve to reveal the ambiguity of some of our own most frequently employed philosophical terms, since profoundly contrasted conceptions of dynamism and of change underlie Indian and Western thought respectively. Western Dynamics, for example, continually expresses itself in setting problems, the single object being generally regarded as a static entity; India, on the contrary, utilizes the fundamental notions of statics in stating its leading questions, but at the same moment conceives the actual object dynamically as passing from its origin to decay, without becoming clearly recognized and distinguished as a static existent separated from other cosmic phenomena—another significant trend of thought suggested by India's tropical Nature. The vast and polar system of Indian speculation, then, regards all things as subsisting side by side, both in Space and Time, all alike being equally expressive symbols of the hidden vital force behind or within them. In the West however, History, the study of singular events and personalities apprehended in their chronological order and relations, is the leading principle. In India, conversely, this singleness of unrepeated occurrences and characters counts for nothing, and thus historical thinking, in its Western sense, never became able to provide any basis in principle. But these and other still more antithetic features of Western and Indian mentality will be demonstrated and illustrated by concrete examples in my later chapters.

The discussion of one and the same group of problems from these two contrasted standpoints, the anthropological and the cosmic, reveals the multitude of widely divergent possibilities. Man's mind, indeed, may be able to conceive even more than these; and it is undeniable that in both cultures alike side-shoots can be discerned branching off from the main stem and appearing, in some cases, to approach the other system. But when we consider the deep elemental differences dividing East from West, all these apparent similarities will be found to be merely accidental. Even if they digress occasionally from the fundamental tendency, the underlying inherited trend of thought still remains extremely effective in spite of the seeming reciprocal approximation of the two different worlds of thought.[1]

But before I continue my comparison between these intellectual domains, two leading questions must be considered together with their many implications. In the first place, then, why select the preceding systems as characteristic types of the cosmic, and the anthropological, standpoints respectively?

[1] *Cf.* Chapter 8.

Secondly, which of the widely varying aspects of Western speculation should be emphasized in eliciting parallels? And to what extent may we regard Western Philosophy on the one hand, and Indian Philosophy on the other, as genuinely consistent and as actual unities?

The last question is not difficult to answer. Owing to her geographical conditions India, to repeat, affords the best example of uninterrupted cosmic tradition. The most important invasion within historic times occurred about 2000 B.C. when the Aryans, whose name means "inhabitants of Iran," descended from its mountain plateau into the fertile plain of Northern India. It is true that these Aryan intruders brought with them an Indo-European language and culture; but it should also be remembered that this Indo-European inheritance had undergone specific changes in Iran itself, where only the Persians and the later Indian Aryans combined to form a cultural unity. The invading Aryans, moreover, found in India an already highly developed culture, the main representatives of which were the Dravidians who are still predominant in Southern India. From 2000 B.C. till about A.D. 1000 there were no invasions of any historic significance; during these three thousand years, therefore, the Aryans consolidated their own imported culture with that of the Dravidians who had preceded them, and together with whom they had to live within the comparatively isolated Indian continent. It may have been the Dravidians who, as already closely adapted to the *force majeure* of India's climatic conditions, assumed the lead in this composite Aryan-Dravidian culture. But be that as it may, when about A.D. 1000 the Mohammedans invaded India on a still larger scale, Indian civilization had become unified to such an extent that it could no longer be changed in any decisive way; on the contrary, these Islamic late-comers themselves fell more or less under the dominating influence of India's natural conditions. This accounts for some remarkable changes which their socio-religious and artistic outlook underwent during the relatively short period of the last millennium; and all the later immigrants who settled on Indian soil were quickly imbued with the cosmic ideas that are so closely knit with Indian Nature, while when the Indian religions themselves spread over to the geographically more open districts of the Far East, the leading Indian cosmic concepts steadily acquired predominance there also. It is sufficient to recall the influence which Buddhism, a genuine Indian religion, has exerted throughout the Southern and Northern regions of Farther Asia, in China, Korea and Japan as well as in Burma, Siam and the Malay Archipelago; in these Southern districts, indeed, not only Buddhism, but also India's Hinduistic religions obtained a firm hold. Thus India can quite justifiably be regarded as at once the most productive and the most conservative centre of cosmic speculation in the Middle and Far East. As to the Near East, it includes no cultural centre that could possibly rival India as regards geographical isolation and its resultant natural connection between soil and thought. The anthropo-geographical standpoint that I have adopted implies, therefore, that the characteristic—unless indeed we should say non-characteristic—feature of the Near East is its geographic, and together with this its cultural, openness to spiritual invasion. Spiritually, that is to say, the Near East has always tended towards the Mediterranean: a principle advanced by Professor H. Becker, late Minister for Culture in Germany and one of the most expert interpreters of Islamic ideas.[1] The Mohammedan countries of the Southern Mediterranean came too early into contact with those of the Northern Mediterranean to prevent an amalgamation with the West. Islamic religion, moreover, has modelled itself upon still earlier monotheistic creeds. Thus the God of Islam is conceived as strictly personal and as, in a sense, the heavenly counterpart of the great personalities of conquerors and warriors on earth. Systematized Islamic rationalism, again, as expressed in Mathematics, the Natural Sciences and Art, appealed to the Western mind as did Western mentality to the Mohammedans, and thus it was possible for the Mohammedans in the Middle Ages, especially those among the Arabs who had never come under Indian influences, constantly to receive and develop, to preserve and return Western

[1] *Cf.* his *Islam-Studien.*

European ideas. We may therefore look upon them as the outposts of Western anthropological thought.

Thus our last question may now be answered in the affirmative: and India, the genuine type of an undisturbed cosmic world, can be contrasted with the West and its leading conception of personalities who dominate and control Nature.

Now let us revert to the other preliminary question: Which systems of Western Philosophy are most suitable for comparison with the East? To answer this inquiry is extremely difficult, and within the brief scope of this volume only an outline can be given of the whole field. I shall be able, however, to indicate the salient features, even though I cannot do justice to the finer details.

I select to begin with, as being psychologically most important, the era of Western Philosophy during which Sophism steadily detached itself from the earlier cosmic outlook, according special attention to Greek Philosophy, and pointing out, still further, those occasional breaches in the Western trend of thought where an apparent *rapprochement* to the impersonal cosmic viewpoint has occurred. I shall deal also with the most recent period of Western Philosophy when profound doubts arise regarding its foundations: doubts, for example, as to the predominant status of the human mind, the competence of Man's reason and the value of individuality. Then, by the way of reaction, a new collectivism emerges: relativity is proclaimed in place of strict dogmatism, biological valuation of dynamic urges is postulated instead of intellectualism, and synthesis is applied instead of discrete analytical investigation. Thus since the days of the Sophists' dogma of "Man as Measure," the Western outlook has expanded to almost a completely new polarity. A new dynamism, a new cosmic philosophy, has arisen or is about to arise.

A further task will be to emphasize the fundamental difference between the presuppositions and problems of India and those of the West during these periods of apparent resemblance. For reaction itself reveals the very nature of action; and as modern anti-individualism has of necessity passed through the stage of individualism, it is therefore totally different from the non—but not anti—! individualistic attitude of India, where the problem of individuality had never been seriously considered.[1]

I must also call attention to what appears to be an influx of Western dogmas into the radically different basis of Indian thought; and in this connection I shall indicate the periods of apparent *rapprochement* between the anthropological view and the cosmic, in order to demonstrate their fundamental otherness. Finally, the analogies which suggest themselves will be investigated in such a way as to reveal their non-analogical background.

From this general standpoint, again, it seems advisable to consider the same range of problems from both the anthropological and the cosmic philo-

[1] *Cf.* Chapter 4 and pp. 94 ff.

sophical points of view; a comparative survey will therefore be undertaken of the development of the various systems of philosophy in East and West respectively. One section will be devoted to Theology, another to Ontology and Eschatology, a third to Ethics, after which I shall deal first with Logic and the theory of perception, and then proceed to Aesthetics. The two succeeding sections will be devoted to a comparison between Eastern and Western Philosophy of Physics, Mathematics, Astronomy, Philology and social problems, and finally I shall consider modern European cosmic Philosophy in the light of the development of similar conceptions in India.

We shall thus discover how unequal were the respective contributions of East and West to each of these domains. Each subject is differently valued in the Occident and the Orient, and has therefore been developed with greater or less success. The West has, for example, and with excellent results, concentrated on the exact sciences—Physics, Astronomy and Mathematics, together with social problems; India, on the other hand, has made more valuable contributions to Metaphysics. In short, the West has elaborated the best systematic framework of thought, while India's natural task is to keep this framework sufficiently elastic to embrace all possibilities of thought, equally those already realized and those not yet foreseen.

Now why is this? A question that I shall attempt

to answer. To begin with, however, the meaning of the term "Philosophy" itself in East and West remains to be investigated; and as I have already indicated, linguistic research discovers facts which yield the clue to the underlying idea. *Nomen* is still *omen*, especially in India's magic world.

Let us examine then, the Western term "Philosophy" and its Eastern equivalent in the classical language of India, Sanskrit; and even at the outset we meet with fundamental contrasts. For the Greek term *philo-sophia* means literally "love of *sophia*," of human reason, measure, of judgment and discrimination. On the other hand, the Sanskrit term for philosophy[1] is *anu-īkṣikī*, the "survey of, literally the look along (*anu*), all things," which means "along all existent facts." Thus contemplation of reality, not discrimination in a rational order, is the cardinal aim of Indian Philosophy, the Sanskrit name of which means no more than synopsis, comprehensive view and receptive contemplation. Further evidence of the profound gulf between East and West is provided by another fundamental philosophical term. Our word "system" (*systema*) is literally "putting-together," "com-position," in a rational order. It was Aristotle, the founder and organizer of Western exact science, a post-Sophistic scholar and the first great genuinely Western Philosopher, who invented

[1] The term *Tarka* is limited to the meaning of logical scrutiny and is rejected by most of the philosophical schools; but *cf.* further, Chapter 5.

the term *sy-stema* or *sy-stasis*, while his school, the Peripatetics, developed it to its full meaning. The human mind, then, thinks "systematically," prescribes the order of research, the selection, disposition and composition of ideas. Conversely Plato, the ontological and, indeed, the last great cosmic thinker of the West, continues under the influence of pre-Sophistic cosmic conceptions to apply to his own principles the pregnant term *theoria*, meaning literally "intuitive view," or contemplation. This use of *theoria*, instead of the later *sy-stema*, reveals Plato's general attitude, his humble openness towards the phenomena as objects of contemplation, but not of selective research.

Now precisely the same concept of "system" as Plato's was conceived by Indian Philosophy and has been preserved to the present day, the Sanskrit term for system being either *darśana* or *dṛṣṭi*, both derived from the root *dṛś* (Greek *derkomai*)—to look, to contemplate, to be receptive—but in no degree implying any idea of regulating the facts of Nature.

CHAPTER 2

THEOLOGY

In the light of this interpretation of the Sanskrit term *anu-īkṣikī* as a contemplative, but in no sense regulative synopsis of facts, it is clear that it is not at all consistent with India's fundamental canon to accept Western post-Aristotelian subdivisions of Philosophy for the sake of comparison. Let us begin, therefore, with the subdivision of widest cosmic range—Metaphysics and Ontology, in which Theology must be included.

In the West, in the first place, the term "Metaphysics" was not originally understood in the special sense which it later acquired, namely that of research transcending all physical facts. Aristotle himself, indeed, usually speaks of Metaphysics as the "first philosophy," and it was a library label that accidentally gave the whole subject its accepted name. For the works that followed Aristotle's treatises on Physics were called τὰ μετὰ τὰ φυσικά, "those coming after the Physics"; but the Greek preposition *meta* merely indicates temporal order, so that the title "metaphysics" did not originally refer in any way to the actual contents of the volumes.

In India, on the contrary, Metaphysics never acquired the significance of "beyond" all physical facts; it has rather always been pure Physics. If then

Indian Metaphysics is concerned with problems centring on the conception of God, that is with Theology, Metaphysics may be called "a second Physics," since God is the heavenly counterpart of earthly physical beings. If applied, again, to cosmic primeval Physics, or to Ontology, then the meaning becomes "extended Physics," while when it deals with the fate of Man after death, it is a "renewed Physics," simply because India's ideas of life after death, of the Hereafter, are those of another "here," of a new life on earth in reincarnation.

I shall begin, then, with the problems of Theology, that is with the fundamental ideas about God in West and East respectively.

In the early scriptures of both Ancient Greece and India, God appears merely as the personification of atmospheric phenomena. The life of the early communities of herdsmen (the so-called patriarchial group) and of the agricultural community (which may be termed the matriarchal group) was chiefly influenced by those elemental facts of Nature on which they depended: the alternation of day and night, the visible signs of which are sun, moon and stars; favourable or adverse weather conditions, thunderstorms and winds, rains and drought. These external phenomena, on which depended the prosperity and often, indeed, the very fate of Man, could not be altered and directly modified by primitive Man. The feeling that he was completely dependent on these outward processes, therefore, rendered Man humble in the face of the uncontrollable forces of Nature. Prompted by a powerful instinct of self-preservation, however, Man attempted to establish some sway over them by worshipping and placating the mighty beings which, he believed, were incorporated in atmospheric forces, by the acknowledgment of their dominion, resigned submission to their authority, and perhaps the utilitarian desire to gain their assistance and favour by satisfying and strengthening them by means of libations.[1] It is this attitude, then, that we invariably find underlying all primitive worship.

Exactly as the principal gods were believed to reside in the upper regions of the atmosphere, so the minor gods were conceived as the inherent powers of all the animate and so-called inanimate earthly things which are of such vital importance to Man and the satisfaction of his countless needs. Thus the early Greeks conceived rivers and streams as inhabited by nymphs, and presumed the existence of spirits in trees and mountains. And just as in ancient Greece, these deities have been venerated in India too since the earliest times; stranger still, the Hindu has clung to these conceptions of deity to the present day; and it is this that accounts for the characteristic cosmic tinge of Indian thought. Another mode of divine worship practised in ancient Greece, and preserved also for ages in India, is the veneration, allied how-

[1] In this connection the frequent *Ṛgvedic* term *vardhayate*, "he causes (the God) to grow," is illuminating.

ever with fear, of powerful beasts; and thus the gods in animal form, the Greek Satyr or Centaur, a combination of Man and animal, have had their equivalents in Indian religions at all times; the elephant-god, the snake gods and goddesses, the vulture-god, or the more beneficent deities who assumed the shape of a bull, a cow or monkey; in the main, symbols of wealth and fertility.

In ancient Greece, however, deities existing in the forms of Man's fellow-creatures within natural phenomena were ridiculed as early as the end of the first period of Greek Philosophy. Xenophanes and Anaxagoras, the philosopher, mathematician and astronomer, discarded with contempt these popular beliefs and enunciated the principle of the one, all-pervading and divine λόγος or ἕν of the Universe. In India, on the other hand, there persisted a long and unbroken tradition of worship of Nature-gods. I remember a modern Indian scientist, trained at Western universities, who met me at the station with his car of the newest type. When we arrived at dusk at his home of unchanged Indian style, at that mysterious hour when day passes into night, he humbly knelt before his household altar to offer his devout prayer to the animal-shaped image of his village god.

But while this conception of deity maintained its dominance over India, in the West it was soon abandoned. For at the very period when the Sophistic outlook was developing, that is about 500 B.C., a single paramount principle was postulated as ruling the Universe, at least by the more advanced Greek thinkers, although the masses remained much longer content with an indiscriminate diversity of gods. Such a marked contrast with the views of the leading intellectuals, which has formed a characteristic feature of the West ever since the days of Sophism, finds no place at all in India, where one sole regulative principle has never yet replaced the embarrassing multitude of deities. Even the *Upaniṣadic* theory of the one *Ātman-Brahman* does not exclude the belief in the manifold cosmic expressions of the Divine.

At the same time, it is true that as early as the era of the *Ṛgveda* (*c.* 2000 B.C.) there subsisted in the Indian mind a deity of universal character who was thought of, however, not in connection with any special cosmic manifestation, but rather as pervading all of them alike: sun, moon and stars, waters and winds, the functions of animal life as well as those of the human mind and morality. On the other hand, this concept of *Varuṇa* interpreted as the one dominant power, as ruler of macro- and microcosm alike, has, remarkably enough, been regarded as an imported Aryan, or rather Babylonian, idea, and therefore as a stranger within the Indian Pantheon itself. But this suggestion need not necessarily be accepted, for while the conception of *Varuṇa* is apparently contrary to India's cardinal dogma of plurality, and seems to substitute a personality for the cosmic forces, actually it is *Varuṇa* who provides the best example of India's comprehensive doctrine of the cosmic interconnection of all and everything. In other words, *Varuṇa* is not an early concept of a monotheistic archetype. For when we examine the *Varuṇa*-hymns closely, we realize that it is by no means *Varuṇa's* personality, but the leading cosmic idea underlying his conception which is the key to the monotheism, or rather monism, involved. For *Varuṇa* is again and again called simply the representative, the child, the servant of *Ṛta* as the cosmic, or dynamic, universal order. Whatever he is said to perform, then, he really achieves by force of *Ṛta*—a term derived from the Sanskrit root *ṛ*, to go, to change. And in this respect we encounter a fundamental departure from Western thought. The Greek term for cosmic order is *κόσμος*, the established, the artistically or aesthetically fashioned order (*kosmein* means literally to embellish, arrange, dispose). It places in the foreground, therefore, one who disposes, one who, from without and by means of rational order, brings beauty into cosmic objects. This sculptor of the world, this artistic *dēmiourgos* of advanced Greek thought, rules the objects according to his own mind, his own standards and plans. *Ṛta*, on the other hand, plainly means the *immanent* dynamic order or inner balance of the cosmic manifestations themselves. The inherent equipoise of cosmic processes, their innate beauty, for example, is displayed in the shining of sun, moon and stars, in the flowing of the waters, in the motion of the winds and in the secretions of animal and plant. By force of *Ṛta* the milk in the cow's udder is produced; by force of *Ṛta*, too, the human brain functions; and so with all other cosmic activities. Behind the dominating idea of this immanent cosmic order, therefore, the personality of its guardian, *Varuṇa*, disappears completely. *Ṛta*, like the later cosmic idea of *Karma*, of action and reaction, manifests itself through all forms and through all periods. Both are self-dependent and universal laws with which no earthly will whatever, nor even *Varuṇa* nor any other god, can interfere. Thus the predominance of *Varuṇa* in the Indian Pantheon is only apparent; as ruler he is merely the servant of a yet higher law which is revealed in the plurality of self-active cosmic phenomena. But there exists in India another apparent Monism which at times seems to contradict the fundamental idea of divine plurality; and Max Müller, in indicating one marked characteristic of the Indian mind, applied to the seeming monotheistic or monistic concepts of India the happy term "Katheno- (not Mono-!) theism." Unfortunately, however, Occidental interpreters of Indian thought, always inclined to resort to the easier way of analogy between East and West, have never accorded sufficient attention to Müller's weighty observation; by introducing "Kathenotheism" he tried to explain a theism which attributes the totality of cosmic and divine functions to various deities in turn (*kathenos*). Thus Kathenotheism is, as it were, a time-restricted Monism.

Other apparent monistic tendencies in the Indian conceptions of God (*e.g.* the later *Bhakti*-mysticism) can likewise be traced to the fundamental cosmic background of natural forces, by which the idea of the pre-eminence of a single dominating personality is excluded. In later Hinduism, on the other hand, the supremacy of one God, either of *Viṣṇu* or of *Śiva*, is emphasized by special sects; at the same time both *Viṣṇu* and *Śiva* are derived from early *Ṛgvedic* minor deities possessing atmospheric significance. Secondly, in these particular sects (called Śivaitic and Viṣṇuitic respectively (both *Viṣṇu* and *Śiva* are regarded as nearly equal in rank while, still further, even when the Hindu concentrates on one of these aspects of deity, he never conceives a single personality of one universal God, in Hinduistic belief therefore, *Viṣṇu* still continues to be a kind of "Kathenotheistic" deity of the *Ṛgvedic* type. From this viewpoint he is a combination of the atmospheric god *Viṣṇu* and of *Kṛṣṇa*, who was probably an old deity of cattle. Alternatively—and this is even more characteristic of Indian thought—the god, as the counterpart of Man, is also subject to the cosmic law of reincarnation. For tropical Nature every day reveals swift changes of form as manifestations of one ever-productive centre; and thus *Viṣṇu* is conceived as being dependent on the law of the so-called *Avatāras*, a reversion to existence down (*ava*) through the long periods of different world formations, and this in an ever-new and always relative guise. It is equally noteworthy that these diverse forms of his divine rebirth are not confined to superhuman or quasi-human types, since *Viṣṇu-Kṛṣṇa* is believed to be reborn as a tortoise, a fish, a horse or as a man-lion (a combination of man and lion), as a dwarf or in any other human shape. Similarly Buddhism teaches that Buddha in his former lives, when he already possessed divine potentiality, took the shape of a tortoise, a deer, a parrot, a woodpecker, a crow or any high or low form of Man.

All these incarnations, again, are regarded as being on the same level, and as applying equally to divine beings and to humanity. Even in the so-called mystic period of the Indian Middle Ages and throughout the era of the *Bhakti*-cult, which has been inaccurately interpreted as Monotheism,[1] this doctrine of cosmic rebirth in all varieties of form was preserved—a fact which proves the existence in India of a fundamental dogma of cosmic plurality and cosmic interchangeability, involving alterations of even divine forms.

It must be observed, however, that there are radical differences between this principle of divine rebirth and the expected reappearance of a Messiah in Western religions. For discarding the non-Occidental idea of the reappearance of a God not only in superhuman or human guise, but also in that of an animal, the very concept of reappearance has in India a quite different significance. It does not imply the unique appearance of the God for the sole purpose of redeeming Man, but is merely the Indian tendency to the

[1] *Cf.* Chapter 4.

abolition of all limitations, associated with the law of decay of all definite form that is involved in the doctrine of divine rebirth; thus any individual shape whatever, even that of a personal God and of a single world, is considered purely accidental and transitory.

Second among the principal gods of Hinduism is *Śiva*. He too has preserved, though in a different sense, India's conception of the Divine as merely representing cosmic forces. *Śiva* is thought of in terms of personal or impersonal symbols, as the constant dynamic power of Nature carrying things onward from growth to decay, being then represented either as a combination of male and female, as *Ardha-narīśvara*, one-half of his body being shaped from head to foot as man, the other as woman, or again in animal shape, as a bull (a symbol of fertility), or merely imaginatively under the twofold symbol of womb and phallus, either combined or separated.

In all these aspects alike, then, *Śiva* is venerated as the representative of the ardent tropical power of generation. A second aspect, however—that of a necessarily destructive power—is also symbolized by the same divine shape of *Śiva*. Thus in *Texts* and their illustrations, as well as in plastic art, we find the highest Being depicted as the principle of destruction: *Śiva*, in both his male and female forms, tramples the world into a shapeless mass, thus providing the material for future world-formations. Regardless of their positive or negative effects, *Śiva* performs his natural functions; and so he is conceived under yet another and equally remarkable aspect—as the patron and the model of all ascetics, of those who, untroubled by the possible consequences of their actions, are content with performing them as a non-egoistic duty.

How profound is the contrast between these philosophical conceptions underlying the Indian concept of deity and those resting on Occidental presuppositions, as established by post-Sophistic Greece and combined still later with those Biblical ideas of the Near East which proved to be congenial to the West! For there is in India no sarcasm whatever resembling that of the Greek philosophers about 500 B.C., when Xenophanes and his contemporaries mocked at gods conceived in animal form. To the Indian mind, on the contrary, beasts are just as worthy an expression of divine Nature as is Man. In India, then, not singleness, but plurality and manifoldness of form and type have been at every period, from early Kathenotheism to the latest conceptions of divine duality or polarity, the adequate expression of God-Nature.

Still further, it is not the unique form, not the dominating *logos* or *nous*, that is postulated as the highest cosmic, and therefore by Western standards, regulative principle, operating for its own purposes and according to its own ideals. For in Indian doctrine no merely spiritual principle can ever be supreme. From the very beginning, on the contrary, the second eternal principle of Matter is on an equal footing with

Spirit or Mind, and this basic Indian idea of the equal valuation of Matter and Spirit may be discerned in the *Upanışads,* those "spiritualistic" *Texts* of early Indian Philosophy, which originated about 1000 B.C. and held sway till at least 500 B.C., since *Upaniṣadic* cosmology teaches that the world originated by *sṛṣṭi* or *sarga,* terms which have been wrongly translated as creation, but which actually mean seminal emission from the supreme body.

The same fundamental recognition of Matter as being an eternal and divine principle equal to Spirit is later expressed in the *Sānkhya* Philosophy of post-Christian times. Here too Matter and Spirit stand side by side as both alike eternal primeval principles. This constitutes an additional and striking contrast to Western thought: for according to the leading *Sānkhya* and *Vedānta* systems it is from Matter, not from Spirit, that all cosmic and specific psychic faculties are derived; Man's intellect (*Buddhi*) is also regarded as an emanation of primeval Matter and not of Spirit.

There is yet another remarkable Indian conception, strange to the West, which is likewise an outcome of the *Sānkhya* system, whose influence on all later Indian speculation cannot be overrated. According to this, the merely spiritual principle is considered as inactive and barren, the exact counterpart of a *deus otiosus* who never interferes, in any way, with cosmic happenings; and this is illustrated by the well-known metaphor of the Spirit riding as a mere passenger in the chariot of the cosmic urge. Everything that happens on the journey then occurs wholly without the concurrence of the highest spiritual principle; the body is the vehicle, the objects are the course, the material sense-organs are the horses, while the intellect, being merely a subtler material substance, is the driver, the Spirit being only a spectator or, at any rate, no more than a master for whom all is done.

Exactly the same meaning is implied by another metaphor dealing with the problem of activity and the possibility of interference on the part of the spiritual principle, in which the *Sānkhyam* describes the highest Spirit as the owner of a bedstead. But he takes no active part in supplying the material; he is no creator; neither does he shape nor arrange it; that is the craftsman's task. God therefore is not even like the Greek *dēmiourgos*; he is only the customer for whom the bed has been manufactured so that he may sleep in it: *deus otiosus*.

According to yet another metaphor of the *Sānkhyam*, implying, it is true, indirect activity rather than complete passivity, God is the magnet attracting Matter, thus causing it to move and influencing its direction, while himself remaining static.

Still another fundamental contrast between Western and Indian conceptions of God is that, for Indian speculation, God is not almighty. Beside him stands primeval Matter, while above him are the two eternal cosmic laws: the eternal law of reincarnation and that of *Karma* which, through all the manifold forms of reincarnation, manifests its efficacy in action and consequent reaction.

In Homer, however, as with the pre-Sophistic thinkers, we discover a similar acknowledgment of supreme cosmic laws: for neither *Moira,* self-incurred fate, nor *Ananke,* natural necessity, is subject to the will or grace of Zeus.

The only right, or rather duty, therefore, which the so-called theistic philosophical systems of India concede, even in later times, to God, is to resemble the earlier god *Varuṇa,* whose task it was to enforce the strict observance of these eternal laws, both by Man's deliberate conduct and by the less conscious, or even purely mechanical, activities of animals and inanimate objects of Nature. Beyond this the logical system of the *Nyāyam* confers upon God the futile function of counting the innumerable atoms.

It is inevitable that this Indian concept of God, or rather the gods, as Nature's representative, should profoundly influence Ethics; and thus the problem which has always been of vital importance to Western systems of Theology, that is whether God, as creator, is responsible for evil as well as for good, finds in India an easy solution. For since God is but the mirror or symbol of a still more dominant Nature, this question becomes wholly irrelevant: it is Nature itself that must exercise the dual power of generation and destruction. These are therefore interdependent: Nature creates while destroying and destroys while creating; and consequently all ethical canons fall outside the range of Nature's laws.

A further dilemma of Western Theology which never perturbs the Indian mind is whether God can possess anthropomorphic qualities, can be a reflection of Man's mind and at the same time be pure Spirit or *Logos*. In India, then, God is divine in all and every shape, even in animal form, simply because every thing without exception is divine in its very essence as being the manifestation of the sacred forces of Nature.

We may now summarize India's conceptions of deity by quoting the emphatic words of the very first *Ṛgvedic* speculation on God,[1] which still remains valid in the latest phase of Indian systematics. "The gods are later, they are on *this*, the empirical, side of the world"; or in other words, they are products of the mechanical and automatic cosmic emanation. Thus India states a problem, and answers it in a very strange way, which in the Occident cannot even be raised, since it is against all our Western presuppositions about God's uniqueness and supremacy to search for His origin, for the source of the supreme Reality itself.

As I observed at the beginning of this chapter, then, Metaphysics in the sense of Theology is in India a second or specific type of Physics, so that while God may be primal with regard to value and to time, still He is not a Being totally different from

[1] *Ṛgveda*, x, 129, 6.

all other universal forms; and in indicating those Indian ideas about God which are necessarily strange to minds habituated to the Western realm of thought, I have endeavoured to make the resultant contrast clear; other questions pertaining to the vast range of Eastern and Western Theology will be dealt with in the later discussions of Ontology, Ethics and Physics, including for example the problem of divine miraculous interference with the course of Nature or History, as exemplified by the familiar Biblical narratives of darkening the sun, drying up the sea to save the chosen people from momentary danger, punishing the Jewish people by sending a foreign king as the instrument of vengeance, etc.

Another group of questions concerns the dogma of divine grace: has India any conception analogous to that of God granting salvation solely in virtue of His divine quality of mercy? Again, is everything in God's power entrusted to His justice and redeeming love? Is "sin" possible against God, or against the cosmic harmony? These enquiries pertain to my chapters on Ontology and Ethics.

Theology, finally, is in general regarded under totally different aspects in the East and in the West: in India beauty and purpose are looked upon as inherent in every cosmic function, while to us they are mere accidentals coming to objects from without; a point to be more fully treated in connection with aesthetic principles.

I may add a few questions from the sphere of the

Psychology of Religion—what is the purpose of confession? Is it nothing more than spiritual relief? Or does confession—in accordance with Indian belief in the law of cause and effect—mechanically result in self-liberation? Or (lastly) is it, following the Western view, but a preliminary stage through which the repentant sinner must pass on his way to final redemption granted by a merciful God?

All this must be considered in the light of the principle that the Indian God appears to be divested of every personal attribute of divine omnipotence, as this is conceived by us, in favour of the integrity of an impersonal law of Nature which neither Man, nor even God Himself, can violate.

CHAPTER 3

ONTOLOGY AND ESCHATOLOGY

In the preceding chapter I ventured to call Indian Theology a second Physics, in order to clarify the Indian conception of God as the counterpart of physical entities in a different sphere though not on any fundamentally different level. This leads to the subject-matter of the present chapter—still in accordance with India's basic doctrine of invariable cosmic existents, Ontology is interpreted as extended Physics, Eschatology as renewed Physics.

In considering the relevant Occidental doctrines, three different attitudes towards the problems of the eternal source of all Being must be specified, which in the course of intellectual development have assumed the philosophic forms of Idealism, Materialism and Realism. The first of these, the idealistic, explains all phenomena as the outcome of one original spiritual principle; the second, Materialism, conceives them as resulting from a primary material principle, while the third, having its roots in the world of realities, recognizes two fundamental principles which are then placed on the same level of value and involve a restricted concept of eternity: this is the doctrine of Matter and Spirit as found in the facts of the world.

What then is India's orientation towards these

leading Western ontological ideas? in the first place, we must recall the significant fact that India has remained unchanged and uniform throughout all historic times, and that she has preserved her own consistent outlook in all her philosophical systems, however diverse these may seem. From this it follows that, in India, the different philosophies can never involve different basic standpoints; and consequently there are certain fundamental presuppositions which are common to *all* these systems. Thus the basal conception of *Karma,* of reincarnation and liberation, is recognized by all Indian thinkers without exception. Wc should not therefore expect to find, in Indian speculation, the three Western dogmas of Idealism, Materialism and Realism, each resting on its special foundation.

It may be asked, nevertheless, which of the three approaches most nearly to the basic Indian view of all Being? To begin with, are India's spiritual foundations consistent with Idealism?

A pure Idealism is ruled out by India's characteristic conceptions of the Divine. For the Indian mind is consistently reluctant to acknowledge the pre-eminence of any unique, original, eternal and active spiritual principle, that is to say of any creator of the empirical world. There is in Indian cosmology no God who, *ex nihilo,* creates the whole Universe by His will and after His own plans. Even in the so-called theistic systems there is always primeval Matter beside Him, and beyond Him impersonal laws like those of *Karma*, *Ṛta* and Reincarnation. Secondly, there is the spiritual principle itself conceived not as an ultimate unity, but as the plurality of the *puruṣas*. This spiritual principle, further, as in the fundamental system of the *Sānkhyam*, is thought of not as active, but, on the contrary, as a barren, or at least as only an indirectly stimulating, principle of all Being. Neither God nor any other spiritual principle, then, is all-creative and almighty.

It might however be supposed that, in place of one God or a plurality of gods, the laws of *Karma*, Reincarnation, etc., to which even the gods themselves are subject, would be regarded as the supreme principles of all Being. But all these regulative laws are impersonal; they do not rule the world from without according to their own imposed schemes, but are immanent in all cosmic phenomena and processes. In other words, they are not external entities existing anterior to world events, but unities which can be grasped only when they become disintegrated and manifested throughout the infinite diversity of cosmic phenomena. The eternal principles of *Karma* and Reincarnation, that is to say, are not pre-existent to cosmic happenings, but come into existence together with these. Neither they, nor the gods, then, can be regarded as the origin of all things. With the merely Abstract the Indian mind never concerns itself, under the dominance of tropical Nature it never loses sight of the Concrete as continually forced upon it by the environing dynamic forces which manifest their active presence in everything; and in the chapter on abstract formal Logic I shall return to this topic.

While therefore these considerations preclude the conclusion that the Indian mind conceives the pre-eminence of an ultimate, unique and single spiritual principle at the beginning, preceding the world, it might still be supposed that India has derived an idealistic Ontology from the doctrine of *Māyā*, which is usually interpreted as that of the illusory and unreal nature of the empirical world. Further, has she not in fact adopted idealistic views in her dogma of the dissolution of the world into *Nirvāṇa* (dispersion) which implies the ultimate annihilation of all existents?

In the first place, however, *Māyā* as the illusion or fiction of empirical reality is to be found only among some of the later Buddhistic and *Vedāntic* sects, *e.g.* the *Yogācāras* and *Śankara*, the "disguised Buddhist." In the West, therefore, its importance for Indian thought has been highly overrated, probably because it chanced to find its most emphatic and eloquent expositors in Schopenhauer and his pupil Deussen, both of whom adopted it as exactly according with their own philosophical systems; and this proves how extremely misleading such analogies between Eastern and Western ideas can be. For as I have observed in my *Introduction*, we are never justified in comparing, and still less in identifying with each other, single doctrines detached from the systems and specific spiritual traditions in which they are rooted. In order to discover the actual meaning of *Māyā*, then, we must investigate its growth within the Indian world of thought; we have no right whatever to select a certain stage of its development, at which it apparently agrees with Schopenhauer's *Weltanschauung*, and wherein the Universe is a mere fiction or only the outcome of human or superhuman consciousness and transcendental Will.

In the first place, we must not overlook the fact that the term *Māyā* occurs in the early and world-affirmative *Texts* of the *Ṛgveda*. There *Māyā* is used in the sense of a merely neutral capacity in good and evil spirits alike, and by no means only as a negative conception as in late nihilistic Buddhistic *Texts*. Nor can we assume that there has been at any time a break in the development of the *Māyā* dogma; this would be unlikely in a firm and continuous tradition such as India's, where the word *nomen* always means "omen." The sense of a noun is enhanced, and at the same time interpreted, by its verbal root, which is often repeated in the same sentence, and to which is added, if possible, yet another derivative of the same verb, in order to secure the utmost significance. It is therefore fortunate that we find the term *Māyā* combined in the *Ṛgveda* with its verb *mame* and a second noun of the same root *mā*, "to measure," in the same verse.[1] In both passages we find *Māyā*

[1] 9, 89, 9; 5, 85, 5.

together with *mānam* and *mame*. Thus *Māyā* is the capacity for measuring, attributed to the multiform (*pururūpa*) gods *Indra* and *Varuṇa*, as well as to the multiform god of *fire*, *Agni*, all of whom can assume any shape. Similarly, in the *Bhagavadgītā*, *Kṛṣṇa is called Māyā-vin*, *i.e.* possessing the capacity of *Māyā*, measuring, when through his *vi-bhūti*, or dissection into all *bhūtas*, all definite beings, he reproduces the world-emanation in all its forms. Through his *Māyā*, then, *Kṛṣṇa* reproduces all types of persons and inanimate objects—a most characteristic mixture! *Kṛṣṇa*, in other words, makes himself manifold in appearance, dissects himself into different forms as *vy-akta* and *vy-āpta* (the prefix *vi* expressing divergence, disjunction). By means of his power of measuring, that is to say dividing, *Kṛṣṇa* assumes all actual forms of the empirical world, manifesting himself as all *viṣayas* (things fallen apart) as all *vyaktas* (things curved apart), in every *mūrti* (solid form), as *pṛthak* (extended Matter), as all *tanūs* (extended or spread-out things). In short, by means of *Māyā Kṛṣṇa* appears in every possible empirical shape; by its means all manifold, all separate, *i.e.* measurable, single forms originate. Thus *Māyā* must be understood in the light of its derivation from, and combination with, the root *mā*, "to measure," found in the *Ṛgveda*. In virtue of *Māyā*, that is through his power of multiformity, the *pururūpa*, either *Indra*, *Varuṇa* or the fire-god *Agni* is called *Māyā-vin*, "possessing *Māyā*." Thus if we derive

Māyā correctly from *mā*, "to measure," we readily find the connecting link between its Vedic meaning and late Buddhistic usage: all *māyas*, all measurable definite things, are then inferior to the *Avyaktam*, to the presumed primeval chaotic and ever-productive mass, as is taught by the *Sānkhyam*. To begin with: all *māyas*, all measurable empirical objects, are smaller, and in consequence of this inferiority in size, they are—in accordance with the Indian equation of quantity to quality—subordinate to the *Avyaktam* in value also. Secondly, the *Sānkhyam* asserts that all empirical objects are emanations from the productive seething mass of original Matter; thus all *māyas* again are inferior, because secondary, in Time, as compared with primeval Matter, the so-called *Pradhānam*, or literally the Foremost, the primeval Matter being an indefinite and limitless complex. Further, every measurable, *i.e.* definitely shaped object, since it has a beginning, is bound to have an end; having been constructed, it is liable to destruction; it certainly has full empirical reality, but is still only definite, *i.e. Māyā*. It is indeed possible to go further and interpret it *sub specie aeternitatis*, as Non-Being, simply because it has no being at *all* times; while since all becoming is later (in the *Yoga*-system and with the *Sarvāstivādins*) regarded as an accidental aggregation of *Kṣaṇas* (moments), every *māya*, all definite form or empirical reality, becomes a *transcendental* illusion, transcendental unreality. The Buddhistic-Vedāntic

Māyā, again, implies that although the objects of the world have definite empirical reality, they do not possess the transcendental reality of the Indefinite.

This explanation of the true meaning of *Māyā*, which deserves to be even more detailed, because it expounds India's fundamental principle so often misunderstood in the West, should make it clear that *Māyā* is unreality not in the transient world, but unreality in the eternal world, since the aggregation of single individual forms can have no static existence, but only a continuity of change. Here then we are concerned with the basic difference between the eternity of a transcendental statics and the continuity of an empirical dynamics, or in other words, the radical contrast between "to be" and "to become."

This doctrine of *Māyā*, however, even in its negative formulation by Buddhistic-Vedāntic sects, is not akin to any Western idealistic system. For in the first place, no superiority of any discriminative spiritual principle is recognized; on the contrary, it is the supremacy of the materialistic, the chaotic, principle that is implied; it is eternal Matter that is asserted, and into this each single form in the end is reabsorbed. But is this dogma of the eternal existence of the primeval material substance consistent with the concept of *Nirvāṇa*, which is generally interpreted as absolute nullity? Now it is impossible, to begin with, to assert about this idea of *Nirvāṇa* what has already been said about *Māyā* as illusion. I have already pointed out that this nihilistic interpretation of *Māyā* is not universally accepted in India, being only one of various possible interpretations of a few late sects. On the other hand, the *Nirvāṇa* concept, though this is rarely realized, is accepted by a wider range of Indian schools than is the *Māyā* conception; and the term *Nirvāṇa*, in its fullest meaning, is a universal Hindu idea, and by no means confined to a few Buddhistic sects. But *Nirvāṇa* never means nullity, either to the Buddhists or to other Indian thinkers. Certainly it is often associated with *Śūnya* which, among other meanings, may have that of zero; *Śūnya*, however, is not always used in this restricted sense of zero, or "nothing," in Indian Mathematics and Metaphysics, since it also signifies the Indefinite; and in early *Texts* of the *Atharva-veda*[1] it appears combined with *Nir-ṛti*, "the non-tendency"=dissolved.[2] In the *Ṛgveda*, again, *Śūnya* occurs as a synonym of *A-bhva*—a polar-paradox term meaning the exuberant or the non-existent. Elsewhere[3] *Śūnya* is connected with the *Aty-antam*—that which transcends all limits. *Śūnya* must therefore be derived from the same stem as *Śūna*, which means "excessive," "swollen," *i.e.* from the root *śu, śvan*. Thus the concept of zero accords perfectly with this idea of an excessive and, therefore, unlimited entity: zero is the non-dimensional, that which cannot be narrowed down to any definite number, whether positive or negative. It is the

[1] 14, 2, 19. [2] Root *ṛ*: to go + *nir*; *cf. nir-vā-ṇa.*
[3] *Cf. Petersburger Wörterbuch sub verbo.*

productive point of potentiality, the starting-point in both directions alike, lying precisely between both groups of integers. Consequently its identification with *Nirvāṇa* is extremely significant: like *Nirvāṇa*, zero (*Śūnya*) is a kind of reservoir which never flows out in one direction only. In this connection the metaphors may be cited that are applied in *Chāndogya-upaniṣad* 6 to the *Aṇutva*, the concept of the immeasurable atom, and especially to the description of the *Aṇutva* as the shapeless ocean into which all streams flow, losing their individual forms and names while increasing the limitless ocean waters. *Śūnya*, therefore, is a term which is polar in its very meaning, or in other words, cannot be confined to one single direction only (*cf. A-bhva* and *Aty-antam*). Thus *Nirvāṇa*, like zero, means not nullity, but "no-thing," *i.e.* the indefinite things; both terms (as well as *Aṇutva* in *Chānd.-up.* 6) mean the same as *Brahman*, the material and spiritual background of the whole Universe, of the entire plurality of world-emanations. Further, this indefinable *Brahman* can be explained only by being defined as *na-iti, na-iti*: "it is not (only) this, it is not (only) that," implying that *Brahman* is the reservoir of all things. It must again be insisted that these concepts of zero, *Brahman* and *Nirvāṇa* are far more than mere idealistic principles; for the reality of all empirical or definite form is never denied, but is on the contrary conceived as being contained in a timeless reservoir that is simultaneously non-dimensional and all-dimensional. Thus at the very beginning, and at the very end, of Time there is no empirical *Bhāva*, no continuous change through growth to decay. There is, in other terms, no "becoming," but there is instead the underlying *Sat*: static Being which has either not yet flowed out, or has ceased to flow, in single emanations. Indian Ontology, therefore, postulates a dual Reality—the empirical Reality of all worldly forms and the transcendental Reality of "form no longer," or "change no longer"; and thus both *Māyā* and *Nirvāṇa* are realities and not, as is generally assumed in the West, unrealities.

According to Indian Philosophy there is indeed, even in our present lifetime and in our stage of definite form, one state in which we may experience this super-definite Being. For in deep dreamless sleep, free from all memory of empirical happenings, we attain the super-conscious, super-rational stage of "no-form," or form that cannot be grasped in any way. Thus we plunge into the reservoir into which all definition and all consciousness are absorbed, but out of which empirical functions may reappear.

In the next place, do these typically Indian ideas about the first and last principles of all cosmic Reality involve Idealism as this is conceived by the Western mind?

In India, it must be observed, this first and last principle is not regarded as being fundamentally different from primeval Matter; it is neither primeval consciousness, nor is it a purely spiritual principle; rather it is Matter itself in its chaotic stage of indefinable fullness or immeasurable emptiness, together with the original urge towards self-manifestation. It is the eternal reservoir of empirical facts, wherein they appear united, or re-united, into a super-conscious phase, thus becoming super-empirical and limitless. To the Indian mind, then, not *logos,* but Matter is the transcendental and, at the same time, the world-emanating principle. Every single form, even that of a divine *Nous,* is merely a manifestation, and is as such bound up with one or several definite, though superior, forms.

And with this we return to what has already been said in Chapter 2 about the possibility of conceiving God in either human, superhuman or animal form; for so long as God is regarded as a "something," He is within the sphere of shape and definition; He is therefore but a symbol, *i.e.* one of the many apprehensible forms. Now all forms without exception, both high and low, both good and evil, are simply aspects of human judgment, and as such are all within the scope of definition; the very Highest, on the contrary, must be beyond it.

Even Matter and Spirit, in fact, are only two aspects of one and the same thing; and thus, by the so-called dualistic system of the *Sānkhyam,* they are regarded as being on the same level in their quality of leading principle, although it is only one of them, Matter, that constitutes the foundation for all universal forms, high and low, fully conscious or only partially conscious, God, Man and animal alike. Perhaps the *Upaniṣads* and the *Vedānta* are in this respect more consistent than the *Sānkhyam*, since in their theory of *Ātman-Brahman* they do not even distinguish between Matter and Spirit, that is between the cause of all material existence and Spirit. *Ātman-Brahman*, as the very first and the very last principle combined, is once more the reservoir from which all emanations originate and in which all manifestations end. Popular Hinduism, however, endeavours to illustrate this philosophical problem of primeval Matter and Spirit by employing metaphors. Nevertheless the personal god *Śiva* is, as such, only a symbol, nothing more than an instrument in the process of world-change, a means of formation and destruction. Worldly forms emanate from his body as almost involuntary secretions (*Sṛṣṭi*, *Sarga*) just as, again almost mechanically, he tramples the world to a shapeless, though formative mass in the *Pralaya*, the process of melting, or coming to (*pra*) a coagulation.

Or is Indian Ontology, since it does not accord with Western Idealism, a theory of pure Materialism?

First, it must be noted, not Matter alone, but Matter and Spirit combined are, according to the Indian standpoint, active at the very beginning and the very end of the Universe. Secondly, there is the fundamental concept of an after-life for all single existents, and even for individual worlds. The

Universe as a whole, that is to say, undergoes the same necessary changes, through growth to decay, as does the least of its constituents.

India, still further, asserts transcendence in the sense of the super-empirical continuity, if not indeed the eternity, of all beings, and also of the world as a whole. It is true that in India a purely materialistic tendency appears from time to time, which assumes that there is only a "here" with no "hereafter." These materialists, however, the so-called *Cārvākas*, have never influenced the general Indian attitude of mind, except by affording a stimulus to all other systems for the discussion and the emphatic refutation of their ideas; and in the diverse philosophical systems that of the *Cārvākas* always ranked lowest among the sixteen that were recognized, lower even than that of those who worshipped the strange metal mercury as a Deity.

Thus although it is true that some Indian philosophers express belief in the existence of elementary atoms (as did Democritus, Epicurus and other Western Materialists), still these atoms are not considered to be purely materialistic, and much less ultimate, foundations. Certainly there is the *Aṇutva* or atom-likeness, already referred to as a metaphysical principle. Thus atoms are never merely material facts; rather do they provide such metaphysical problems as that of dimensional relativity. They are symbols of the non- and the all-dimensional, a metaphor for *Brahman*, and must thus be regarded as mathematical and metaphysical, rather than materialistic, conceptions. It is also true that the *Vaiśeṣika* system—that of the different empirical categories (*Viśeṣas*)—propounds an atomic theory combined with a theory of the four, or rather five elements water, fire, air, earth and *Ākāśa* (ether) as the quintessence. But behind these elements and atoms lies the primeval Matter-Spirit of which they are only the first emanations; and in this way Indian materialistic atoms are always traced beyond the empirical world.

As to the after-life, we find in India a singular combination of Ontology and Eschatology, that is of the science of Existence and the science, or rather theory, of an after-life. Thus India conceives Eschatology as renewed Physics, a renewed life on earth. The *Saṃsāra* (derived from *sar*) is a continuous stream of actual lives, and should never be rendered as the "*cycle* of rebirths," since the individual in its rebirth never returns to the same, but always to a more developed stage of incarnation, in accord with the growth of its own inherent tendency. All Indian thinkers hold that the *Karma-bīja* (*Karma* seed) biologically develops into the *Karmaphalam* (*Karma* fruit) thus choosing for its next embodiment a more adequate and less limited form of existence.[1] The life after death, therefore, which according to some doctrines is interrupted by a transitory stay in the sun or moon, in heaven or hell (later doctrine), always

[1] *Cf.* further my chapter on Ethics.

leads back to another incarnation on earth; the "hereafter" is only another "here."

This, however, is not the final goal of Eschatology, concerning which India's conceptions may, following Mrs. Rhys Davids' suggestion,[1] be subdivided into *Anchistology*, the theory of the proximate phases of the after-life, and Eschatology proper, the final stage wherein ultimate absorption of all personality takes place, even the vague individuality preserved by the *Karma*-bearer during his various stages of reincarnation being swallowed up by the indefinable *Nirvāṇa*.

But in both cases alike India attained what may be called transcendental Materialism. For while genuine Materialism conceives the world as one unrepeated formation India, on the other hand, rises above single empirical observations and postulates the transformation of one empirical form into another, and finally of all these into a static shapelessness which is beyond all empirical experience; and this, once again, precludes the identification of India's Ontology with Realism.

Thus behind the given empirical phenomena of psycho-physical duality and psycho-physical parallelism there subsists, as the final goal, the specifically Indian cosmic idea of the transcendental polarity, as well as the unity, of both Matter and Spirit in the Indefinable.

[1] C. A. F. Rhys Davids, *Indian Religion and Survival*, pp. 96 ff.

India, then, may well be compared and contrasted with the West. All her concepts are concentrated around, and directed towards, one central cosmic idea which magnetically attracts all diverging speculations in *one* direction—towards the dual goal of polarity and limitlessness. This is the consistent cosmic outlook tending towards ultimate oneness—the real *Uni-verse*—that is towards the primal and final *Sat*, static "Being," which can nevertheless be grasped only in its derived forms of transient "Becoming" in the empirical *Bhāvas*.

CHAPTER 4

ETHICS

THIS chapter is concerned with the many and difficult problems of Individuality, and of individual right and duty.

In the first place we must consider two different concepts of Individuality: that of India's cosmic Philosophy and that of the anthropologically determined West. In India, then, the individual is always part and parcel of the Whole. Man, most closely woven into the universal cosmic network, is subject to precisely the same biological laws of growth and decay as all other forms. Thus he is neither biologically nor axiologically singled out from all other universal manifestations. Under tropical conditions such as India's, the sole canon of value is vitality as revealed not only in Man, but also in powerful beasts and prolific vegetation. But what the human mind gains in spiritual energy it is bound to lose in physical vitality, since there operates a secret law of the cosmic balance of forces, so that an increase in any one direction is nearly always associated with a consequent compensating loss in others; over-development of one capacity, therefore, inevitably results in the crippling of others. According to India's cosmic outlook the individual does not stand in splendid isolation; he is not δεινὸς ἀνήρ, the all-powerful Man, of ancient Greece.

On Man, then, many strata of cosmic manifestations weigh heavily, so that he is at once impressed and oppressed by the diversity of cosmic phenomena. Celestial lights and atmospheric conditions limit human possibilities, and even form the basis of religious worship.[1] On earth, too, Man depends on extra-human circumstances: animal life either threatens, or supports, his own, while the success, or failure, of the crops determines human prosperity or misery in India's unmechanized civilization; and thus it is that eminently practical considerations have plainly influenced some so-called ethical laws. Perhaps a utilitarian reason underlies the fact that India punishes damage to animals, and even to trees and shrubs, more severely than the West, and this in order to compensate not the owner but the damaged plant itself!

But not only extra-human entities influence Man's life. For the ideal of humanity as a totality, as this has been recognized in the West at certain periods, and also the ideal of obedience to the authority of the State, as embodied in a king, are not ideals which govern the life of the orthodox Hindu, both being more or less irrelevant to traditional India. The ideal of mankind, in the first place, is excluded by her isolated geographical position,[2] just as the ideal of submission to political authority and to its single

[1] *Cf.* Chapter 2.

[2] *Cf.* the Indian cosmographical maps which centre around *Jaṃbūdvīpa* (India).

personal representative is scarcely compatible with an orthodox Indian's indifferent attitude towards all transitory personalities and historical events. At the same time other forms of authority, of a more permanent character, must be associated with India's typically biological canon. Of these the most prominent and powerful is the permanent dominance of the caste. The caste system, however, is not a socio-political institution to the degree that it is generally held to be by Western interpreters, who naturally follow their inherited trend of thought, but is regarded, to begin with at least, from the biological standpoint. For just as everywhere in Nature, especially in animal groups such as ant and bee communities, the Hindu perceives a kind of biological division of labour, so caste too is considered to be an institution the purpose of which is highly specialized spiritual and physical breeding by means of restricted selection. In the early *Texts* of the *Ṛgveda* and *Brāhmaṇas*, again, where we first encounter the idea of caste, the divisions imply no social classifications; rather is human society compared with a huge organism functioning through the balance and co-operation of all its members. Thus the Brahmins or priests are regarded as the head, the second class, the warriors, as the arms, while the *Vaiśyas*, or trading and agricultural classes, are the trunk, the fourth and lowest caste, the servants, forming the feet of this gigantic organism. It is expressly declared, however, that no part of the Whole may claim exclusive importance and superiority over the others. The undisturbed collaboration of the Whole is what matters, and thus all parts become equally necessary within the single system of co-operative labour; in this way the microcosm of the caste system is the lesser counterpart of the cosmic macrocosm.[1]

The Indian view of the status of the individual is most clearly exemplified by that tricky toy, the Chinese puzzle boxes, in which a series of boxes is fitted one into another, so that a larger always encloses a smaller. The smallest of these boxes, then, represents the individual, enclosed in many "cosmic" environments and, indeed, almost disappearing under them. The greatest, on the other hand, would be the celestial Cosmos, enfolding the extra-human terrestial cosmos, which in its turn would include within itself the caste. Within the caste, still further, there are other subdivisions to which the individual is closely bound—the limits of the joint family restricting not only the freedom of decision of each of its ordinary members but also that of the natural head, the *pater familias*; and in this connection it is noteworthy that Indian traditional law does not permit the unrestricted disposal of property. Inherited and personally acquired belongings are the common property of the joint family, and even the head is but the temporal manager and the representative of an impersonal authority to which he himself is responsible. In exactly the same way the family

[1] *Cf.* my earlier discussion of *Ṛta*.

proper—father, mother and children—depend in their personal relationships on impersonal and, once more, biological laws. Strict sex ethics, or rather hygiene, is prescribed, confining marriage within the narrow bounds of the caste, and at the same time prohibiting it within the same family, the definition of prohibited sex affinities being very wide, and indeed influenced at times by considerations of magic. For instance, a man may not marry a woman bearing the same name as his mother, since there is believed to exist between them a magical relationship which would render sexual intercourse incestuous. There are in addition all the other marriage regulations, including those relating to child-marriage and the fate of the widow, and all having a biological-ethical trend which severely limits the personal wishes of the individual in the name of impersonal hygienic responsibility. The status of the individual within his environment is thus strictly defined, not so much however by other individuals nor by State authority as by impersonal biological, or in other words cosmic, laws.

How very narrow, then, are the limits circumscribing the individual! Nevertheless, he possesses definite cosmic influence as one of the innumerable cogs in the Universe's machinery; each person has his own specific status, duties and rights assigned to him, and bears his due share of cosmic responsibility. In this connection my deductive method of philological-philosophical interpretation may be once more employed; the Indian term for duty is *Dharma*, or in the *Ṛgvedic Texts Dhāman*, both of which, when rendered literally, mean "the fixed position." *Dharma* therefore is (1) the fixed position of duty and (2) at the same time of right; in short, the sphere of function; as such, still further, *Dharma* is not restricted to the range of personal ethics, but (3) also designates religious observance and (4) even secular law, prescribing the individual's legal standing within the wider domains of the community, caste and State. Finally *Dharma* is (5) a general principle, or law of Nature, involving in addition the psychological doctrine of the Buddha; in other words, *Dharma* is everything that is fixed, or to which the individual is bound; and this in a twofold sense, both positively and negatively, by deriving from it support (*dhar*!) and obligation alike. Thus *Dharma* is duty and right simultaneously; and as universal order it assigns to each individuality—be it personal or impersonal—its specific place within the wider community. A final consequence of this conception of *Dharma* is found in Buddhistic logic, where all phenomena, all fixed and definite objects, are called *Dharmas*.

In its cosmic, and not simply individual, range, however, and owing to its dual meaning of ethical duty and right, *Dharma* can be identified with none of the Western concepts of duty. For while it imposes on Man obligations towards non-human beings, it is by no means akin to the Christian idea of obedience and humility towards Deity, since *Dharma* prescribes not only the acknowledgment of obligations towards a higher, a supreme Being, but also towards lower beings, and this again not as a mode of indirect worship of a creator. *Dharma*, moreover, is not only negative obligation, in the guise of the restraints of duty, but is equally the sustaining influence of right; self-preservation and the preservation of fellow-creatures, therefore, are equally sacred aspects of this mutual cosmic contract. Nor can the Indian *Dharma* be identified with the Greek socio-ethical concept τὰ ἑαυτοῦ πράττειν—the fulfilment of civic duty, which only the "idiot" (*i.e.* the non-political, unsocial *idiōtēs*) neglects. Much more extensive than this, both internally and externally, is the range of *Dharma*, since it inculcates duty not only towards those intimately associated within the family nor, in the Greek sense, to socio-political bodies such as the caste or the political community, nor again towards all our fellow-creatures on earth including the less animate forms of plant life, but also towards the inanimate constituents of the cosmos. All this is part of the cosmic contract of balance from *Brahman* to a tuft of grass or post (*Brahmādistambaparyantam*). India's concept of duty, therefore, is far wider than ours; Man is not merely the Aristotelian *zōon politikon*, but *zōon kosmikon* too, and thus the significance of *Dharma* is profounder than that of any of its Western equivalents. The law of Indian duty admits of no exception whatever; no God, no Nietzschean "superman" can claim exclusion. Nor, again, does the law of *Dharma* in any way resemble the ethical necessity of the Stoics, which implies that Fate, or predestined duty, leads the willing but compels or, literally, drags the unwilling: *Fata volentem ducunt, nolentem trahunt*. *Dharma* is rather the idea of universal justice, involving responsibility in its widest sense, not, however, in the guise of any external compulsion but as immanent necessity, so that all that has ever come into existence produces its specific reaction or effect—the law of action and reaction as laid down by the principle of *Karma*, which is no ethical dogma in any Western sense; nor is it a doctrine of reward and punishment, though generally so regarded, and still less is it comparable to the Western law of "measure for measure" (*lex talionis*). For the fully developed *Karma-phalam* (*Karma*-fruit) by no means corresponds in size to the small *Karma-bīja* (*Karma*-seed). It is therefore not the static law of the correspondence of deed and reward, but the dynamic-biological law of development and growth, that forms the presupposition of the *Karma*-doctrine. The word *Karma* simply means activity; in the philosophical *Vaiśeṣika* system it denotes the category of motion, thus comprising both activity and its aim; grammatically it is the accusative, the direct object of action. The so-called ethical *Karma* theory, therefore, is not Ethics in the Western criminological sense of protecting the social community by punishing and segregating the offender; it involves no act of justice by a revengeful God nor —semi-indianized—retribution of the impersonal *Karma*-force. Nor, again, is *Karma* self-inflicted punishment in Schiller's sense of the curse of foul deeds consisting in their generative power for further evil. It is purely biological ethics, revealed in the inviolable law of cause and effect, and imposing on the individual a super-personal responsibility towards both the future and the cosmos.

This means, still further, that the main tendency of character becomes manifested in the later stages of rebirth in forms better suited to Man's intrinsic needs. Thus even rebirth as an animal is not necessarily degradation nor punishment, as is abundantly clear in the varying incarnations undergone by the *Bodhisattva* in Buddhist *Jātakas* or birth stories, and similarly in some Hinduistic *Texts* dealing especially with the subsequent series of reincarnations.[1] This enables us to compare India's theory of *Karma* with two cosmic principles of early Greece—first, Aeschylus' tragic curse upon successive generations, and (secondly) Plato's dogma, in his *Republic*, of the free choice of reincarnate form granted to the dead; both are parallel, though in different ways, to *Karma* theory. Aeschylus, it is true, proclaims punishment rather than any ethically indifferent law of causality; nonetheless is the concept of a tendency continuously operating throughout generations the same in both systems. For it is no single incarnation that is

[1] *Cf. e.g.* the *Viṣṇu Smṛti*.

responsible for the act; rather the deed itself, or the psychic predisposition thereto, is regarded as being transmitted, for the Greek tragedian, by physiological heredity, and in the case of the Indian *Karma*-bearer by psychical inheritance. Similarly it is often asserted that Plato's idea of reincarnation was derived from the Indian concept of *Karma*, which had by various paths diffused into Greece. Nevertheless there are marked contrasts between the Indian doctrine of reincarnation and the Platonic free choice of destiny which the soul enjoys during its intermediate stages; at the same time it is not the factor of free selection that distinguishes the Platonic belief from the Indian, since this is in one sense recognized in India, too, because the inherent tendency of individual character determines the form of the succeeding embodiment. Still further, both India and Plato accept the essential idea that punishment never accounts for rebirth; for since India's ethics is cosmic-biological, the inevitable consequence is that every action is bound to its due reaction. Neither "good" nor "bad" therefore is an ultimate canon in India's natural, in the sense of ethically indifferent, Philosophy. But while both are merely relative, still the power of development in any given direction is irresistible; and this introduces an additional specific dogma of Indian Ethics, equally strange to the West, regarding the evaluation of sacrifice. For the writer of the *Ṛgvedic* sacrificial hymns exalts the sublimity of his "Kathenotheistic" god, while at the next moment addressing to him the strictly business proposal that he should give his worshipper, in exchange for his hymn, his *Soma* or honey libation, cows or children, although this *do ut des* principle—"I give that thou mayest give"—of the early *Ṛgvedic* period is stigmatized by Western interpreters as an immoral transaction. On the other hand, the idea of a contract between the devotee and the object of his devotion persists through all the later developments of India's cosmic thought systems. Secondly, the ethics of the sanctity of contract is involved. For each act generates its own inevitable consequences; it is both the effect of some preceding action and the cause of its successor. Thus the outpoured energy, whether in the concrete form of a gift or, more abstractly, as will and thought expressed in a hymn of praise, is a sacrifice (*Yajña*), and later philosophical *Texts* of the *Upaniṣads* and the *Bhagavadgītā*, etc., distinguish different types of *Yajña*, such as sacrifice in meditation, or procreation, speaking or breathing, etc. In short, all expended energy is regarded as concrete substance which, when directed to some object of devotion, increases its force, thus enabling, and indeed compelling, it to achieve adequate counteraction. From the same viewpoint the doctrine of *Bhakti* must be considered. Literally *Bhakti* means not devotion offered to a single God, but reciprocal participation, its verbal root being *bhaj*, "to share, to partake, to enjoy" (*cf*. also its intensive form, *bhakṣ*, "to consume"); and thus it is a later expression for the earlier sacrificial magic or sacrificial partnership between God and Man, which again is based on the natural law of cause and effect.[1]

Nothing therefore can ever be lost, since everything causally produces an effect which will in turn again be cause. In this sense, then, Indian Ethics is natural, biological. It is true that in Western post-Sophist days the Stoics advocated the principle of "living in accordance with Nature," which certainly presents some degree of similarity. They add, however, that the source of good is Man's rational capacity, so that the Stoic doctrine implies no recognition of any cosmic duties. According to the *Ṛgvedic Varuṇa*-hymns, on the other hand "*Ṛta* commands the winds to blow, the waters to flow and Man to know," so that exactly as the unconscious or partially conscious constituents of the Universe fulfil their specifically assigned duties, so Man should become clearly conscious of his own position and take his proper place as one party to the cosmic-social contract, all mankind being, as it were, but a caste that has been invested with special capacities involving special duties, and set at the summit of the cosmic organization as one member among others which are less conscious of their respective functions.

But the Stoics' formula, "Live in accord with Nature," acquires wider meaning when it is associated with their other ethical doctrine of *adiaphoron* —the ideal of indifference towards good and bad,

[1] *Cf. Synthesis*, pp. 99 ff. (Paris, 1936).

pleasant and unpleasant, alike. This approximates to the Indian standpoint; and Eastern influence on the Stoic systems has actually been discovered. In the first place all natural functions, as such, lie beyond ethical judgment. *Śiva* the god generates and destroys, both activities being *Sat*; and it is indeed possible to summarize the whole of Indian Ethics by considering *Sat* from the philological-philosophical point of view. For in accordance with Indo-European linguistics *Sat* is merely the present participle of the root *as* (Greek *asti*, Latin *est*); *Sat* therefore means "Being," but in India *Sat* also means "good": whatever exists, in other words, is justified by its very existence. If now the compound of *Sat*, *Satya*, the *Sat*-like, is taken into consideration, the fundamental Indian ethical principle becomes clear; for not only is all Being *Sat*, good, but as such it is also *Satya*, "real" and "true"; and hence every dynamic expression of life, simply because it is life, is true and good.

This interpretation serves further to elucidate the Indian standpoint regarding the moral ideal of asceticism; and it is quite incorrect to say that India has advocated the ascetic ideal as applicable to all persons and all ages alike. The direct contrary, in fact, is established by the very definition of *Sat* itself, and equally by the entire later *Āśrama*[1] system which concerns the so-called three, and subsequently four, religio-social stages of life. Thus according to the natural necessities and demands of youth, manhood

[1] *Ā-śrama*, "coming to rest."

and old age respectively, socio-biological law governs the life of the orthodox Hindu. For youth, therefore, as the stage of mental receptivity, the *Āśrama* law prescribes the study of the sacred *Texts*. In manhood, on the other hand, the practical activities directed towards generating and maintaining a large and prosperous family are commanded; and not until a grandson is born and the continuity of the family in this way assured, may the Hindu return to his early studies in order to deepen them and transmit them to his descendants or pupils; only thus will he attain satisfaction. For now he has come to rest (*Āśrama*), to *Nir-ṛti*, non-tendency; all desires having ceased, he is content (*sam-toṣa*, lit. "to silence oneself"), monk-like (*Muni*, the "silent"), having no wants, asking for nothing; and so the Hindu is *Muni* at every phase of life, while satisfying its imperative demands. The paramount ideal of Indian Ethics, therefore, is to be throughout life a useful member of the widest of all communities—of the Universe in all its dynamic processes.

What then is the duty of Man? What answer does philological analysis suggest? To begin with, Indian terms for moral conduct are strikingly few: they are *Dāna*, "to give to others their due," *Dayā*, "to sympathize with our fellow-creatures" (lit. to "share," *day*, from the root *dā*) and finally *Dama*, "to restrain one's passions," because every urgent desire that finds expression may expand beyond all limits. Still further, all these ethical qualities are comprised in the single *Ahiṃsā*, or abandoning the wish to damage or harm,[1] by infringing in any way the privacy of our fellows.[2]

More specifically, however, *Ahiṃsā* includes the right and the duty of self-defence, and thus becomes something more than a merely negative attitude, since it is actually an active participation in the manifold aspects of the cosmic contract which involves an impartial guardianship of the rights of all parties thereto.

Another extremely significant term which is generally translated "compassion" occurs in the *Taittirīya-upaniṣad—Sam-vid*,[3] or "con-science," "con-sciousness" in its widest sense of being aware equally of one's own and of others' rights, consciousness not as the triumph of human reason but rather in the sense of the analogous *Ṛgvedic* term *Kra-tu* and the later *Kar-uṇa*, both derived from the same root *kar*, "to fulfil one's function." *Samvid*, therefore, means "to know, to find the connection, the contact, the contract with others." This will recall Man's specific task of being conscious by force of *Ṛta*, the universal functional order.

The Buddhist ethical term *Maitri* (from *Mitram*, "contract or neutral friendship") is another expression of the same tendency towards cosmic balance

[1] Skt. *han*, Gk. *phon*.

[2] *Cf.* my exposition of the wide aspect of *Ahiṃsā* in *Bull. Bhandarkar Institute*, 1931.

[3] *Sam* = Lat. *com*; *vid* = Lat. *scio*, "to find, to know."

and justice. But *Maitri* cannot be identified with *caritas*, doing good for its own sake, disregarding the personal merit of the recipient; for it implies no personal concern nor indiscriminate kindness towards all, but objective justice, the assignment of the proper position (*Dharma*). There is nonetheless a certain moral content in this indifference, since it is manifested not only towards evil inflicted upon others, but also towards all that happens to oneself.

Finally, the crucial Occidental moral problem of free will calls for consideration. While India does not regard the will as being determined and predestined by God, there is nevertheless a type of inner determination, or rather immanent predestination or predisposition, in that the individual is inseparably bound to his own almost mechanical law of self-development, in the sense of the realization of its most powerful impulses. With this is associated the old dilemma whether the soul is a *tabula rasa*, or whether on the contrary there are "innate ideas," which agitated the Western mind from the Stoics to the English Empiricists. India advances the solution that although the soul is certainly not a *tabula rasa*, at least not from the beginning of any single incarnation, still it has no innate ideas in the static sense, since its inborn predisposition steadily grows, and is therefore dynamically subject to continuous change.

And thus the conclusion is reached afresh, that India's Ethics is biological and cosmic.

CHAPTER 5

LOGIC

THE first verse of the *Nyāya-sūtras*, the so-called Formal Logic of India, runs as follows: "By understanding the essence of the norm and the object of knowledge, of doubt and motive, of example, dogma, syllogism and scrutiny, of discrimination, discussion, disputation, intrigue, sophism, trick, the futile answer and the flaw in argument, by all these sixteen foundations of logical argument the highest religious aim of liberation is attained." Regarded from the standpoint of Western logical method, this miscellaneous programme certainly contains some strange features; side by side appear many subjects which Occidental Logic tends to distinguish from one another much more definitely. The psychological theory of perception, which involves methodical investigation into the sources of knowledge, stands on the same level as the syllogism, which pertains solely to Formal Logic; while not only are the purely theoretical bases of discussion dealt with, but also its practical applications; and still more surprising to the Western logician is the aim of all this intellectual activity, which is regarded as having not merely an epistemological objective, but at the same time the non-rational and religious goal of spiritual liberation.

On the other hand *Anu-īkṣikī*, Philosophy, is the

general science[1] which does not involve specialization, and therefore erects no subdivisions whatever; and even in its so-called Formal Logic India never emphasizes the arbitrary order dictated by the human mind; nor are abstract theoretic investigations separated from their practical results; finally, Logic itself has a religious or cosmic aim, which it shares with all other disciplines of similarly general character —that is to extend the limits of reasoning and thus to transcend the narrow bounds of the individual mind. Thus understood, Logic provides a way to liberation from that isolation which is, to the Indian spirit, only an illusion, *upādhi*, or attribute that is projected into the objective world by Man's subjective rationality. Whatever truth may be, it is gained by escaping from fictitious subjectivism and in this way attaining objectivity.

I shall first of all consider the sections of this *Nyāya* programme dealing with theoretical Logic, beginning with the *Pramāṇas*, the canons or criteria of truth. In this respect the Indian mind recognizes different norms of knowledge from those known to the West, and at the same time assigns different values to those which East and West share in common. In the first place the Indian logician, like his Occidental colleague, accepts proof by means of the sense-organs, or so-called direct perception, selecting for this the significant term *Praty-akṣam*, "reference back (*prati*) to or towards the eye," visual knowledge

[1] *Cf.* Chapter 1.

here representing all the senses. From this starting-point, sense impressions themselves are never subject to doubt; whatever we see is true and yields infallible perception. Theory[1] is therefore receptive seeing; the sense-organs while receptive are both efficient and sufficient. In other words, truth emanates not from the rational and discriminating mind, but is implied in the objective facts themselves, and only if they remain intact can truth be discerned. According to Indian speculation, then, it is the objects themselves, not the organs, that are active in the process of perception, and for this reason they are called the *Ati-grahas*[2] or supreme agents of perception, while in the *Kāṭhaka-upaniṣad*[3] they are regarded as phenomena of an order higher than the receptive organs. According to Indian theory of perception, objects emit a subtle substance consisting of minute membranes composed of superficial pellicles, which travel to the eyes and the other sense-organs, impinge upon them and spontaneously combine with another subtle substance emanating from the organs themselves, if they are intact—a hypothesis which was advanced also at a certain period in ancient Greece. Thus a kind of real bodily image, *eidōlon*, of the object itself is produced; and because this is part of the object, it is fully as real as the thing itself is. In this connection it is noteworthy that in India terms like "grasp," "conceive," "perceive," "understand," etc., have

[1] *Cf.* Chapter 1.

[2] *Bṛhadāranyaka-upaniṣad*, 3, 2, 1.

[3] 3, 10.

retained their complete and literal meaning, and even late commentators on the systematic philosophical *Texts*, such as *e.g.* the *Nyāya-bindu*, emphasize the plasticity of these expressions by applying to them synonyms that have been formed *ad hoc* and derived from the functions of ordinary life; thus *prati-panna*, generally rendered by "understood," literally means "having approached." Every approach to a thing, that is to say, is grasping it; and since the process of perception is real, it must be effective. In Indian Logic, therefore, there is no scepticism with regard to that knowledge, acquired through the senses, which constitutes empirical science. Indian science, in fact, though it became systematized at about the beginning of the Christian era, and so long before the microscope was invented, has neither changed essentially nor readily submitted even to-day to the influence of Western technics—a subject to be reconsidered in my final discussion of India's attitude towards the *Yantra*, or technical, "magical" instruments.

And as I have already observed in Chapter 4, the term *Sat*, "Being," implies by its very acknowledgment of existence a valuation of truth and goodness; whatever exists is true and good, simply because it exists, and there can be no doubt whatever as to the reality of existence itself. Actual objects, then, possess reality and are therefore called *māyas*, measurable definite forms;[1] whence it follows that

[1] *Cf.* Chapter 3. *Pra-māṇa* is literally rendered "measuring towards."

the act of perceiving these realities is itself real and inevitably achieves the desired effect.

In addition to the foregoing *Pramāṇa*, as a criterion dependent on the senses, or rather the objects of sense, there is the second proof attained by inference; and the terms for inference, *Anu-māna*, *Smara* and *Smṛti*, again possess great plasticity. *Anu-māna*, then, should be rendered "to measure along," by employing the measure already acquired from the preceding direct impression of the *Pratyakṣam* or direct perception. All *Anu-mānas*, still further, are *Smṛti* or *Smara*—memories of the direct impressions caused by the contact between object and sense-organ; the value of inference, therefore, is always dependent on that of direct perception.

The third *Pramāṇa*, *Upa-māna*,[1] is the criterion of truth by means of analogy, which also has a somewhat different value from that assigned to it by Western logicians who regard analogy as one form of inference; the Indian, however, considers it as an empirical association of two or more similar data; and this analogical proof plays a strikingly important part in Logic, since everything in India is on a common level and essentially alike, the tendency to identify apparently different objects being therefore always operative.

Besides the logical canons that are common to

[1] *Upa-māna* is literally "the measuring of one to another" that is already known.

both Indian and Western Logic, India has advanced a fourth and distinctive method of proof which finds no place whatever in Occidental Formal Logic, although it is a factor in Western religions. This *pramāṇa*, which is accepted in some form or other by all logical schools, is the *āpta-vacana* or *śabda*, that is the assertion (*vacana, vāda, śabda*) of an *āpta* or authority. It may be traced back to the first *pramāṇa*, being as it were direct sense perception of the expert or, on a higher level, of the truth of the holy word or sound. Either the sacred *Texts* of the *Veda*, in the so-called orthodox systems, provide this canon of truth, or the founders' teachings are accepted, by the Buddhistic and Jinistic sects, as authoritative axioms requiring no further argument. In other terms, whatever authority proclaims is truth, either in the religious sense of revelation or in the magic sense already frequently referred to, since whatever is conceived with the productive power of will and conviction inevitably produces a new reality as the concrete substance of the expended energy.

Thus all four Indian *pramāṇas* concerned with Theory of Perception rest on the belief in the reality and effectiveness of all the processes involved—nothing is lost and nothing goes astray; the senses and the power of the word (*akṣaram*)—all these alike are secure bases of *pramāṇam*.

I may add a few remarks on the second logical category of the *Nyāyasūtras*—the character of the object. Once more the term itself reveals its underlying meaning. In Sanskrit the words for objects are either: *nāma-rūpa* or *viṣaya, mūrti, tanū, pṛthak,* etc. *Nāma-rūpa* therefore means that objects can be comprehended by means of the name, the logical-magical aspect, or the *rūpa,* the visible shape, the first principle being based on the presupposition that *nomen est omen,* that is to say, words are *satya,* Reality, and *akṣara,* constant, inviolable entities; for India's magical positivism assumes that an object's name is the key to its very essence, while the second possible approach to things is through *rūpa,* their visible form.

Thus the very terms for object (*viṣaya, tanū, vyakta,* etc.) themselves disclose empirical Reality and not merely some logical label: *tanū,* the extended, *pṛthak,* the spread-out, *vyakta,* the thing "curved apart," or singled out and thus manifested, *mūrti,* the congealed, solidified, *viṣaya* (from the root *si* + *vi*)[1] the single object separated, or literally un-tied, from the group, so that it can be perceived under some definite shape: all these terms mirror empirical facts as being the foundations of Indian terminology, and are derived most probably from observations of the geological conditions, especially from India's earlier volcanic phenomena; the Deccan, the central region of India, was one of the oldest of all volcanic areas. Memories of these prehistoric geological conditions still linger in the Indian mind and are expressed in the names of things, as well as in its concepts of

[1] *Cf. Petersburger Wörterbuch sub verbo.*

Cosmology and world-formations and Indian art, especially in that of the Deccan.[1]

The actual facts, therefore, underlie India's Theory of Perception; and in exactly the same way, the so-called Formal Logic of India, as expressed in the syllogism, never loses sight of empirical Reality. For while the Western syllogistic forms, as enunciated by Aristotle and developed by the Stoics and still later philosophical systems, tend merely to theoretical exposition and to pure deduction, the Indian syllogism is intended first and foremost for practical use. To begin with, it serves to explain to others what is evident to oneself, and thus a didactic purpose underlies all Indian Formal Logic. Secondly, the method of argument also tends to practical means and aims. Still further, the Indian syllogism consists of more than three propositions; the first is the *pratijñā*, the assertion: *e.g.* "On the hill there is a fire." The second, the *hetu*, the visible, empirical and never merely abstract reason for the assertion: "For on the hill there is smoke"; while the third, and the most important from the practical viewpoint, is the *udāharaṇam*, the applied example or examples: "Where there is smoke, there must be a fire, as in a kitchen." The fourth link in this ratiocination is the *upanaya*, literally "bringing near" the thing in question, or the application of the example, which is really nothing more than the repetition of

[1] *Cf.* Chapter 3, and my article, "The Absorbent Power of Hindu Religions," *Journ. Soc. Study Relig.* 1936.

the visible reason as a teaching device: "On the hill there is smoke." Finally, the fifth part, the *ni-gamanam* or conclusion, reverts to the assertion providing its affirmation: "Therefore there is a fire on the hill." This rather surprising method of inference by means of a repetition of the visible reason and the insertion of practical examples (*e.g.* "as in the kitchen") shows which facts are really important to the Indian mind even in "abstract" Logic, the abstract idea being always elucidated by concrete illustration and comparison.[1] The Indian syllogism, then, is not, as with us, an affair of pure deduction, but a sequence of inductions; and it is characteristic of India's practical outlook and its practical conception of proof that not only some positive example, but generally one or more negative examples also, are inserted.

A further and equally remarkable difference from the Western syllogism, still more expressive of India's appreciation of empirical facts instead of abstractions, is implied in the concept of *linga* and *lingin*, the logical Characteristic and its bearer. The European deduces this Characteristic from some general idea which is exhibited by its individual possessor, thereby assuming that the general notion is prior to its manifestation in the single object. The Indian logician, on the other hand, does not approach even logical reasoning from the angle of abstract generalization, but always proceeds from the empirical object

[1] *Cf.* the entire literature of *Laukika-nyāyas*.

perceived, inferring from this some perceptible property and concluding that the unseen object which he seeks must possess this too. To revert to our example of smoke and fire: smoke, the visible object, is the property, and the unseen fire is its bearer; and in this way India never leaves the ground of empirical Reality even in its syllogisms.

This close proximity to the real world, however, is sometimes stressed so heavily as to amount to remoteness from the actual facts. Thus the Indian regards the perception of an object in a certain place as being a concrete empirical process, but he regards in an equally positive sense the non-perception of a thing in its accustomed place whenever the eye returns disappointed from its fruitless search. In this way Indian Logic elaborates its apparently abstruse and highly abstract theory of the empirical reality of non-existence, the so-called positive proof of the negative or non-existence—the *a-bhāva*.

The enumeration of the different modes of discussion constituting the final categories of the *Nyāya* system would seem a mere eristic and futile logical game, were these not so deeply rooted in India's general outlook; but as a fruitless logical play upon words they would be of no value whatever to the Indian practical mind. Their importance arises therefore from their applicability and use and their didactic demands; and from the earliest period of Indian thought discussion has been considered the most effective of all means of scientific research. Still further, the magical belief in corporeal substance, and thus in the efficacy of words, gives deep significance to an exposition of the various methods of discussion, since the slightest error may have irreparable consequences.

Another apparently abstract theory, developed especially by the logical schools of Jinism, arises from the same extra-logical purposes of Indian thought. The Jains, then, have enunciated the strange theory of the five- or sevenfold Reality of things. In the first place, the so-called *syād-vāda* is the assertion (*vāda*) that objects have every kind of potential existence; a thing can therefore be imagined either (1) to exist or (2) not to exist, or (3) not to exist in the present, but to be of potential existence in so far as it has existed in the past or will exist in the future; its existence, again, is considered as dependent on the existence, or non-existence, of other things connected with it. But all these modes of possible existence were not conceived and advanced for the mere pleasure of logical sophism; rather do they reflect India's empirical conviction that no object whatever has merely static existence, but that it is subject to continuous dynamic change both in itself and in its relationship to other things.

What seems at first sight the further abstractness of Indian thought again leads back to concrete empirical observations. I have previously referred to India's love of polaric expression; and the polar meanings of zero, *aṇutva, nirvāṇa,* etc., as absolute fullness and absolute emptiness respectively, show that India has conceived the idea of that which transcends all definite form. This characteristic reluctance to accept the ideas of singularity, definition and static existence is based on the empirical observation of tropical conditions; here nothing whatever stands in isolation, nothing is seen as static and unchangeable; on the contrary, all real forms are moving towards the polarities of destruction and generation; and thus India's polaric thought is much nearer to actual life than is Western thinking in terms of specific rational categories. This inevitably results in a fundamental difference between Indian and Western Logic. To us thesis and antithesis are separate principles; to the Indian mind, however, they are not only not opposed to each other, but necesarily constitute two aspects of the same thing; and I have pointed out elsewhere that Indian antitheses are always correlated and are merely two aspects of one and the same situation.[1] India, therefore, does not employ the Western logical category, "either-or" (*autaut*), but "this as well as that" (*sivesive*).

From the same standpoint may be discerned another characteristic of Indian Logic. As the Latin *terminus* suggests, all logical terms are only arbitrary "limits," not to be found in Reality, but merely rational categories imposed on objects by the discriminating reason. India, however, never abandons

[1] *Cf.* my *Studien zur Eigenart indischen Denkens, passim,* and especially pp. 193 ff.

her empirical basis of thought, and thus Indian terms are not definitely fixed, but are simply approaches along different directions to things themselves, and designed to express their essence by both rational and non-rational methods. In the first place, from the rational viewpoint, every object is connected with innumerable others; every term therefore links any given thing with an indefinite number of others. India, however, does not claim to be able conclusively to outline a thing, but rather tries to fill up from within the whole domain of its activity. Thus to the Indian mind an object's sphere is a combination of innumerable sectors of circles to which innumerable other things also belong. In the second place, India is never satisfied with grasping the essence of things in terms of their rational contents alone; each term therefore possesses, besides its rational, several non-rational meanings. Sound and rhythm, for example, reproduce the psychological impression of the word, which is equally an integral part of the thing together with its rational meaning.[1] From this angle then we must consider the entire literature of *rasa* and *bhāva* in Indian rhetoric (*Alaṁkāraśāstram*).

Since Formal Logic thus involves practical observation, Indian Logic presents difficult problems to the Western thinker; in this respect it is sufficient to refer to the many methods of interpretation applied

[1] For further details of the significance and interpretation of Indian terms and their non-rational features *cf.* my article previously cited, *Synthesis*, p. 94 ff.

by the Western mind to the fundamental dogma of Buddhistic Logic.[1] This rests on the so-called *pratītya-samutpāda*, the dogma of interconnected coming-into-existence, or the interdependence of all actual facts, constituting a kind of chain of causal links lying on different levels, and pertaining therefore to widely different systems of thought. Thus the *pratītya-samutpāda* teaches that age and death are consequences of birth. Birth, again, is a result of dynamic change, which is itself due to the tendency to actual life; this in its turn is an outcome of the thirst after real objects which originates in an innate sensation arising from contact with such objects; this contact is the tendency of the sense-organs, while the senses are based on *nāma-rūpa*, *i.e.* name and visible form; these emerge from consciousness, consciousness from predisposition, and this, finally, from *avidyā*—fictitious isolation or failure to rise above single empirical manifestations. These, then, are the twelve links in the interconnected chain of actual existence; and while psychological, biological and logical elements are all interwoven into this doctrine of causality, they are all alike empirical factors.

Since Indian Logic, then, is essentially practical, it cannot be estimated by any merely abstract criteria but takes its own standards from different spheres according to practical necessities. Indian Logic, both

[1] On this point *cf.* my Review of E. Senart's Translation of the *Bṛhadāraṇyaka-upaniṣad*, *Journ. Roy. Asiat. Soc.*, 1937, pp. 501 ff.

the Formal Logic of the syllogism and the Theory of Perception, is concerned with practical facts, and attempts to elucidate the conditions of actual life into which Man is born. In India's tropical world of thought, therefore, that scepticism concerning actual facts which is so marked a feature of other philosophical systems, originating in climates which exert less dominance over the human mind, never arises. Western Sophists, on the other hand, adopted a sceptical attitude towards perception, in accordance with the anthropological principle: "Man is the measure of all things." By thus elevating Man above other cosmic beings, they isolated him and conferred on him a responsibility which he proved too weak to bear; for the same reason the Sophists proclaimed perception to be unreliable, rather than established by objective facts; and Plato reproached them for their bias towards questioning accepted values and in this way disturbing their balance: *τὰ ἥττω κρείττω ποιεῖν*, "making the less the more." The Sophists, however, did no more than their successors have done by giving human reason arbitrary power over objective facts. Descartes, for example, doubted the reality of the external world and asserted, as the primary certainty, the existence of a thinking subject, *cogito ergo sum*, just as long before him Socrates taught his "Know thyself," *γνῶθι σαυτόν*; both principles alike mean: Make your own *ego* the starting-point for all investigation. The Indian, on the other hand, firmly rooted in the actual Cosmos, never doubts objective facts nor the certainty of all perception, which is to him an objective action due to contact between sense-organ and dynamically active sense-object; equally there is no dubiety in his mind as to the reality of *Māyā*, of measurable and definite forms.

At this point it may be objected that against this realistic view there stands the principle of *Avidyā*—that all actual facts are based on non-knowledge. Like *Māyā*, however, *Avidyā* must be interpreted in a quite different sense from that generally accepted. *Avidyā*, it is true, concentrates on empirical phenomena; but, like *Māyā*, *Avidyā* is only the fiction of the actual world in so far as all things are taken as separated in their diversity. We must accordingly free ourselves from the illusion of an *ahaṁ-kāra*, an isolating individuation which is, be it noted, according to the *Sānkhyam* a superhuman fiction, not merely psychological but cosmic. For in the Cosmos too we assert egoism or egocentrism as soon as we introduce the concept of any mode of isolation, and we return to innate, true knowledge, to primary *Vidyā*, when we abandon this false discrimination between things; in other words, we must become aware of the unity behind or within the embarrassing manifoldness. *Vidyā*, true knowledge, is the synoptic vision of the whole; it is genuine "con-ception," "gathering-together," "con-sciousness" in its literal sense of "knowing-together" all things however apparently different and divergent. *Avidyā* then, like *Māyā*, is the fiction of separation.

Yet another term may serve to elucidate the real foundations of Indian Theory of Perception. *Tarka*, discriminating and dissecting reasoning, is never[1] the final method of conception; this either precedes, or follows, rational reasoning, while in both cases alike there is humble receptiveness towards actual phenomena and open-minded contemplation of the Universe. The first stage is empirical contact with objects, the last is the super-rational perception of the unity immanent in all manifoldness; and this final, most intense and highly intuitive concept is believed to be attained in ecstasy or mysticism. Ecstasy, in the literal sense of the Greek term *ekstasis*, means to escape from one's own rational and definite position; in this sense it has the same aim as mysticism, although each approaches it from a different angle. *Mueo*, in its original Greek, was a technical medical term meaning "to unite," that is to join together the edges of a wound, and was subsequently used in the more general sense of "re-joining whatever has broken apart"; thus *mueo* may mean either to close the lips or to shut the eyes. Literally, then, mysticism means: combining things which had been separated, so as to restore their primal unity. Under this guise mysticism is to be discerned in all the fundamental ideas of India. Original unity, original *Vidyā*, must be

[1] Not even in Indian Formal Logic; *cf.* the previously cited schema of the *Nyāya-sūtras*.

regained; it is this genuine mysticism that is contained in Indian concepts, not the type which occasionally appears in the West. Remoteness from the actual facts is not the basis on which mysticism rests in India. On the contrary, India's very nearness to life, and the concrete empirical observation that every thing in Nature is intimately associated with others, explain India's urge to mysticism. It originates in no spontaneous momentary elevation above perception, but is attained by experimental and gradual progress, springing from the uninterrupted observation of the likeness between all things. Indian mysticism, therefore, is the final result of exact induction, of *pratyakṣam*, of contact with the object; and thus objective mysticism tends to the same end as subjective *ekstasis*. For this transcends the assumed limits of personality, so that restoration of the original unity is the aim of both ecstasy and mysticism alike; each is a different aspect of one and the same tendency to re-unite; neither accepts isolation.

And so we revert to the quotation from the *Nyāya-sūtras* at the beginning of this chapter. All sixteen categories of the so-called Formal Logic of India may be considered as one path towards final liberation; none of them ever isolates Logic from the actual world and removes it to any remote sphere of abstraction; all alike originate from contact with the empirical world. By the contemplation of Nature's diversity therefore, and not by means of isolating definition and rational reasoning, they attain the goal of unity and of final liberation from the fiction of isolated existence. And thus India's conclusion is not *cogito ergo sum* but: In spite of my reasoning I exist just as do all other accidental manifestations of the primeval unity. Everything is rooted in static Reality, that vast reservoir from which all emerges and in which everything will be finally immersed, thus relapsing into immanent and genuine unity.

CHAPTER 6

AESTHETICS

THE Occidental definition of "Aesthetics" is the philosophical, or rather mainly psychological, theory of the "Beautiful," "Beauty" again being regarded as what is satisfactory or pleasing to the aesthetic sense of at least a considerable number of normal spectators. This pleasure or satisfaction, still further, may arise from the appreciation of the reciprocal harmony of forms, or of the harmony between form and matter. Distinct, however, from this pure contemplation of Beauty, there is a pleasure, not merely aesthetic, which arises from the consideration of purposes that transcend the sphere of Art itself. Thus the satisfaction derived from the contemplation of Beauty, as such, may be enhanced by realizing the practical applicability of the artefact and the uses to which it is put. "Beautiful" then becomes the equivalent of "useful." Or, again, Beauty may be enjoyed owing to certain external associations which it suggests; for instance, its connection with moral or religious ideas may yield satisfaction; here Ruskin's definition of the beauty of a work of art, as dependent upon religious and moral conditions, may be cited;[1] and then Beauty is enjoyed as the counterpart of the divine perfection implied in the Western idea of

[1] *Modern Painters*, "Of Ideas of Beauty."

God; Art products give an impression of infinity or unity, of repose or symmetry, as qualities of divine proportion that express God's justice, purity and energy. Thus the work of Art reflects that human striving after perfection which is completely absent from the relativities of actual life, elevating the contemplative spirit far above the imperfections of an existence without repose and coherence. Beauty is also discerned in all the diversity of the phenomena of Nature, unity and symbolism springing from the artist's synthetic experience. Zola, as we have already observed, defines every work of Art as "an aspect of Nature perceived temperamentally," that is to say by the artist's integrative personality. In other words, the aesthetic spectator of Nature selects, from the infinite manifold of actual phenomena, those upon which he confers a supernatural unity.

Now which of these motives has provided the incentive for the creation of works of Art in India? And what type of impression does Art produce on the spirit of the Indian spectator?

In answering these questions it must be remarked, in the first place, that there are in all Indian Art certain restrictions that affect the artist's own personality. For in this continent science, poetry and sculpture have been transmitted, from age to age, in the main anonymously; nor again can the founders of most of the philosophical systems be discovered, since either no individual name has been preserved, or it is so common as to be worthless as a clue, while all family or caste appellations refer to their holder's hereditary functions, and are consequently names of types rather than of individuals, and only rarely is any biographical detail added which might distinguish the individual from the wider circle into which he was born. This is, of course, wholly in accordance with the Indian principle which sets all single events and personalities within the cosmic frame of continuous reincarnation and specific activities. Similarly with Indian Poetry, which presents quite insoluble problems to the Western historian of Literature; while in Indian architecture, sculpture and painting the artist remains still further in the background. An additional limitation which concerns the artist's personality arises from the very nature of Indian Art, since according to the precepts of the ancient Indian treatises the artist is forbidden all free choice of his subject. In poetry, therefore, as in the plastic arts, it is never novelty that constitutes the aim, but rather endless repetition and the minute variation of the traditional. This again is an outcome of India's inherent and strictly conservative appreciation of only few and invariable standards. Exactly as all philosophical systems concern themselves through the ages with a limited number of fundamental problems, so India allows no wide range of artistic problems nor representative forms. A further restriction, or more correctly an extra-artistic basis of all Art, is due to India's general outlook which precludes any isolation of the various disciplines. Indian poetry, for instance, has the task not only of pleasing, but also of informing, and the great epics are at the same moment treatises on law, philosophy and religion, lengthy discussions on these being frequently incorporated. Conversely, long chapters of poetry and mythology may be found in many technical treatises on law and history. In the same way the plastic arts serve other than their immediate purpose, and are never purely aesthetic in the sense of the Western dictum, *l'art pour l'art*. In India, on the contrary, Art is never a purpose purely in itself, so that no artist may create simply according to his own plans; he is never free to choose his subjects but restricted to matter which is either supplied from outside the aesthetic sphere or, if indeed it belongs to this sphere, has already been dealt with a hundred times before. In other terms, both a creative artist and a world-creator are concepts wholly strange to the Indian mind. Every artist must take into consideration factors over which he has no power nor choice whatever.

But is not the sole criterion of Indian Art its usefulness or applicability to life? Even this principle—the external purpose of the artefact—cannot be applied without substantial qualifications. Firstly, the didactic purpose of poetry is based not merely on practical aims, since its primary task is to assign poetry its proper place within the general outlook. Not only therefore should rhythm serve to render the dry subject-matter of knowledge more acceptable to mind and memory, but poetic form as well as content should tend to constitute a single whole; and precisely the same may be said of plastic Art. Here the absence of any secular or purely aesthetic goal is even more striking. In ancient India, as also in later Hinduism, no magnificent buildings were ever erected for secular purposes. Indeed, not before the Muslim period do we find works of art serving any profane or socio-political ends, and until that era smaller or larger huts were regarded as quite sufficient to meet all human needs in a tropical climate such as India's. For religious purposes, however, gorgeous temples and great images of the gods were erected. Handicrafts, it is true, were practised from the earliest times and their products, serving religious and secular purposes alike, express in their symbolic ornament general cosmic ideas and show in their elaborate construction that, for the artist, they must have possessed an importance far greater than that of any mere ephemeral utility. It must further be clearly realized that, in India, every profession acquires mystical significance simply from its connection with the sacred duty of caste; while from yet another angle the immediate purpose of the artefact is not aesthetic. For to the Hindu, Beauty lies not in any harmony between matter and form; and after their original production in some adequate material forms are often reproduced in some other medium which suggests a wholly different expression. Thus we find in Indian architecture in stone many specific forms which are obviously derived from earlier carvings in wood or ivory, or again from ornaments engraved on gold or some other fine materials. In the same way the charm of drama, for the Hindu, consists in a beauty springing from another sphere, such as lyrical poetry or the dance; and in this connection it is remarkable that the two Sanskrit terms for drama are *nāṭakam*, "dance," and *sangītakam*, "a group of songs."

Indian art, then, never has its purpose in itself alone, in the sense of mere harmony between form and matter, nor does it express any purely aesthetic laws of Art prescribed by the wholly unrestricted will and method of the artist himself; but, on the other hand, Indian art never serves one single external purpose.

But is there in Indian art any transcendental purpose such as Ruskin refers to? Has it an aim that is creative, the counterpart of that of a supreme creative Being? Does it reflect absolute beauty and perfection of form, conceived as attributes of a harmonious personality? Ruskin's definition of Art certainly resembles India's concept in presupposing an inherent symbolic value; on the other hand, the Western idea of "harmonious personality," introduced by Ruskin, is undeniably strange to the Indian mind. Its canon of aesthetic value is neither found in the artist's limited and mundane personality, nor implied in the qualities ascribed to divine selfhood. There is, indeed, no actual end constituted by purely aesthetic value, since the artistic form is determined by the material used, or rather by the material in which it was originally conceived; and to this, again, external form is of but secondary importance. It is therefore the psychological impression, associating the artefact itself with some general ideas, that really counts. The multiformity and motion depicted reflect the dynamics and diversity in Nature, which eternally conflict with the recognized qualities of a controlling and harmonizing personality.

This canon is also applied to Indian poetry. Here, too, both objective measure and subjective response are derived from the general outlook, and to this poetry's apparent end in itself is subordinated. As more than 80 per cent of the population still live in rural surroundings, the Indian has preserved an intimate contact with natural phenomena, animals and plants; and from this source have sprung both the aim and the uniqueness of Indian poetry. Its richness in metaphorical expression results from the land's natural and social conditions, and in the systematic treatises on poetry no less than thirty-two different kinds of metaphor are enumerated as modes of comparison between Man and his environmental forms. We may therefore quite rightly trace the Indian's special proficiency in lyrical and allegorical poetry, in fairy tales, animal-fables and aphorisms to his life in the jungle. For the eye and ear of the jungle-dweller must be keen and ever watchful of the constantly threatening dangers; and this faculty of close observation has been especially favourable to lyric poetry, finding copious expression in the subtle variations and differentiations of Indian metre and rhythm, in phonetic assimilation by means of delicately suggestive combinations and repetitions of hard or soft consonants, light or dark vowels. All these complex phonetic-psychological effects are studied, taught and explained in elaborate treatises on poetry to the authority of which every poet submits. In respect of its contents, again, the range of lyric poetry is wide, but at the same time determined by the rules laid down in these didactic works. There thus appears at all periods a lyrical art which depicts natural phenomena, personifying and glorifying them, while the subjective lyric, concerned with love and erotics, has had at all times a prominent cosmic tinge, all the visible beauty throughout the cosmos being lavished on the description of the beloved. So, too, are religious and moral poetry, and even recent political literature, but varied aspects of the one lyric art which in its essence is cosmic-erotic, an outstanding example being the political song *Bande Mataram* in praise of the beauty and charm of beloved Mother India.

In the same way the Hindu's peculiar gift for aphorism is rooted in his *Weltanschauung*. For him nothing ever stands alone; everything is in one way or other typical, and is consequently a recognized truth that can be thrown into the briefest possible aphoristic form; here again the single expression is the representative of the whole. Thus the close contact with animal life is mirrored in the many animal tales which passed from India to Aesop, the father of the Western fable; while there are also systematic treatises on the typology of elephants, horses, etc., as the counterpart of human characterology. In the same way inanimate matter is personified, for example in allegorical dramas in which King Fever wages war against King Health, or King Faith fights against King Unbelief and his auxiliaries, all these being simply the poetical expressions of India's world outlook, since in the cosmic reticulum Man is closely interwoven with all animate, and even so-called inanimate, forms of Being.

A last word on Indian drama: this too differs characteristically in scope from all its Occidental varieties, since it has no aim resembling that of its Western parallel. The Greek term *drama* means "action," and accordingly Western drama has for its object the exaltation of a personality, the sufferings and final perfection, the struggle and victory of a hero. But this kind of *hybris*, of human self-righteousness, is wholly strange to the Indian mind, and its drama is mainly *nāṭakam* (dance), and *sangītakam* (a series of lyric songs), dramatic action itself being considered of secondary importance. Recently, however, Rabindranath Tagore, under the influence of Western categories, has introduced tragic or dramatic problems; but Indian tradition assigns no value to personality, nor is it moved by the triumph or the downfall of a hero who is merely one transitory cosmic figure among innumerable others. For the traditional Indian world knows nothing of socio-psychological problems which, were Western standards falsely applied to Indian conditions, might arise from the ascetic ideal or from certain institutions such as polygamy or the fate of the child-widow. The Hindu, as has already been remarked, readily submits to impersonal duties and to drastic limitations of his own personal wishes for the sake of the whole. The charm of the ancient drama, then, lies in the connection between its content and the traditional epics, together with its lyrical ornament which appeals directly to his delicate phonetic sense and subtle musical temperament. Thus there is no "action," since all Indian drama is meant to be no more than a presentation of typical representatives of all classes of people, and of God and Man in their mutual relationship. In other words, the human drama is the mirror of the cosmic, with its vast diversity of action and function; everything has rights and duties of its own and arouses our sympathy in equal measure by duly carrying out its assigned activities. All Indian art is the mirror of Nature, and the artist has no right to simplify, and so to correct, Nature's manifoldness in order to adapt it to his own ideal plans of symmetry or justice.

The same tendency is obvious in plastic art. When religious places are anything more than mere open spaces of crude natural formation, the edifices are distinct attempts to concentrate Nature's exuberance in the architect's creations. The *Gopuras* of Southern

India—literally the towns, or confined areas from which cattle (*go*) are driven to pasture—represent in their carvings the manifold forms of Nature, gods and animals, human and other figures being depicted in embarrassing richness. Another characteristic of the *Gopuras* is their emphasis of the horizontal line by repetition, thus confining the beholder's thoughts to earth instead of directing them to a higher sphere, as under the arched roof of a Gothic cathedral.

In the next place, the *Gopuras* open directly into the surrounding countryside. Places of worship are never isolated from the wider cosmos but, on the contrary, absorbed within the vaster unity of sacred Nature. Indian architecture, therefore, far from being an end in itself, is content to provide the frame for an essentially cosmic worship. No chamber devoted to a cult, but at the same moment cut off from the outer world, could ever accommodate the masses of Hindu worshippers: it would involve a restriction altogether strange to Indian religious sentiment.

The cave-grottoes of Central India are yet another expression of the cosmic laws that dominate Hindu religion and art, their large inner cult-room appearing to lead to the very centre of the earth. Erratic blocks, moreover, are preferred for religious buildings, because their natural shape needs only slight alteration to suit them for either small temples or representations of huge animals as objects of worship, like the cow and the elephant sculptures in Mamallapuram and elsewhere. In other temples, such as those at Ellora and Pushkar, one rock is left unhewn among others laboriously carved, precisely in order not to impair the inherent connection between places of Man's devotion and virgin Nature herself; while a further proof of the cosmic (as opposed to human) laws that govern India's religious art consists in an irregular complex of buildings being preferred to one regularly shaped edifice for Hindu worship, in accordance with the principle that, in Nature, nothing ever stands alone.

Thus just as natural diversity and irregularity form the leading canons of Hindu architecture, so again with natural dynamics. We need only indicate the peculiar style of temple cars used in Hindu rites, and the carving of wheels to be found on many temples throughout India, both alike being expressions of the dynamic tendencies inherent in Indian art as reflections of ever-changing tropical Nature.

Isolated sculptures, similarly, and again in accord with India's *Weltanschauung*, do not play so important a part as do the grouped forms which occur either carved in the geological strata, or separately from these, and it is equally noteworthy that most of the detached figures are chiselled in the living rock itself. Still further, in order to create the impression that the body of the image is growing directly out of the stone some parts, such as the middle or lower regions of the body, are not sculptured at all, but represented by a mere mass of unhewn rock. Here Nature herself takes the place of a temple as a worthy setting for religious worship, while in other cases the isolated image is set in the vivid life of the jungle and is thus re-absorbed in the landscape, as with most of the Buddha figures in Ceylon and Burma. Yet another psychological-aesthetic principle, derived from the profound tendencies immanent in Nature, is expressed in Buddhist and Jinistic sculpture by the figures being repeated in endless rows of the same or similar type, as a representation of Nature's fundamental law of plurality, which admits only of type and never of individuality. Thus the historic Buddha attained divine rank neither in doctrine, nor in its plastic representation, until he had been placed in a series of similar forms with other Buddhas of the past or future or of different aspects of his own personality.

Although exhibiting definite likeness to Nature herself, those reproductions of the human form can hardly be regarded as natural in which a human body and an elephant-face are combined, or a human head and a snake's body, to express that fusion of cosmic forms prescribed by Indian mythology, which has never died. Divine figures, too, are occasionally represented as uniting specific male and female attributes, and this vertically, not horizontally, as did the Hellenistic hermaphrodites; or again one figure has many heads and arms as symbolic of Nature's manifold functions and dynamic manifestations; or, lastly, the horror of grotesque demons vividly depicts Nature's fierce destructive power.

To the Western eye, undoubtedly, the outcome of all these extra-aesthetic considerations must often appear inharmonious and inartistic. Goethe, for example, in spite of being a great admirer of the rich imagination evidenced in Indian fairy tales, expressed his disgust at these "childish and grotesque elephant-temples, sinister throngs of troglodytes and mad confusion of ornament" of Indian art. Some products of course may satisfy Western taste, but this can be only a secondary and almost accidental effect, as in the case of the wonderful calm, the supreme harmony of some figures of the Buddha. Here the ultimate objective is not beauty, but rather the psychological expression of the underlying doctrinal ideals.

A final characteristic of Indian Art is that in addition to reproductions of human figures or animate life in general, amorphous emblems are employed as religious symbols, highly involved geometrical drawings being regarded as adequately representing Nature's manifoldness and complexity.

A few words on Islamic art in India, which may rightly be called the outpost of Western art,[1] may here be added. Originally Islamic standards were not affected by influences emanating from a luxuriant tropical environment; the whole culture bears the indelible stamp of one strongly centralized power, of

1 Chapter 1.

the belief in God as personal and unique; and the Moghul rulers initiated an era of personalities, perhaps the first in Indian history that may be rightly termed "historical," though preceded by at least three thousand years of pure Indian culture. It was, however, essential for Islam to consolidate and at the same time to glorify the might of the conquerors by raising strongholds and magnificent palaces all over the country; and the mosques are the religious expression of this sense of domination. Mausoleums, too, were erected to immortalize individuals and personal attachment to them. Thus love of God and love of Man were equally expressed in symbols of earthly power. In Heaven, as on earth, strong personalities were the objects worthy of devotion.

It is true that Islamic faith forbids the development of a "personal" cult in its literal sense. The mosque therefore bears no figured ornamentation whatever, only the words of the *Qurān* being illustrated by volutes and arabesques. One central and reasoning will dominates the entire mass and makes the building appear a systematic whole. Even the floral ornaments on the walls, ceilings and doors of mosques and palaces never show the unrestricted natural exuberance of Hindu carving; there is no such intricate representation as that of tropical creepers in a virgin forest found on the *Gopuras* or on Buddhist buildings. The very flowers of Islamic Art are conventionally treated and wrought into a geometrical formal framework. Even when, under later Hindu influence, Moghul Art shows some appreciation of the natural beauty of flowers, it still remains Western in the way it represents these as single objects, and in its floral ornament it never attempts to approach nor imitate the natural exuberance of jungle vegetation.

The sharply defined right-angle and square, again, are features of all Islamic Art, the ornament being here carefully devised and subjected to systematic order. Islamic architecture is the clearly conscious creation of some dominant artistic personality, and accordingly the names of the men who commissioned and executed it are inscribed; while in the case of the Taj Mahal, the most famous of Islamic ornamental edifices, it is believed that Western architects were called in to assist in the work. If so, they would readily have attuned themselves to Islamic mentality, and thus been enabled to collaborate in a way which would have been impossible for Western artists if invited to deal with Hindu architecture.

It was inevitable still further that Islamic architecture should give rise to a type of symbolism strikingly different from that developed by Hinduism. Both Hinduism and Islam, it is true, teach humility towards the supreme Powers. But while the former reduces Man to insignificance by confronting him with the bewildering grandeur of natural phenomena, its great rival achieves the same result by leading him into the overwhelming void of unadorned space. In the wide and lofty mosques, then, Man feels himself minimized and humbled in the presence of the invisible God: similarly in the uncanny spaciousness of a Moghul palace the visitor feels unsafe and helpless, an intruder constantly watched by a thousand invisible eyes.

Islamic architects, again, unlike their Hindu colleagues, avoided the immense and indefinite proportions and mysterious darkness of grottoes and palm forests, and erected their fortresses on some commanding hill-top, and within this are usually the mosque and palace, the audience-hall and mausoleum, completed by crowning domes, whose mighty curves are calculated with mathematical precision.

Here Man does not even try to adapt himself to his natural environment, but rather subjects this to his own ends. Islamic architecture utilizes high and cool marble walls, fountains and bathing pools, all carefully designed in exact geometrical style; the walls are regularly set with windows, whose clear-cut ornamental grating admits the air while it softens the sunshine; and thus Islamic architecture created in India an atmosphere of Western comfort and hygiene.

In both Hindu and Islamic styles, therefore, the line of distinction between the fundamental psychological tendencies of the two cultures, placed side by side by Fate in India's sharply defined continent, are to be clearly recognized: the sober, rational and geometrical standards of Islam, stressing systematic order and dominated by the central idea of an almighty God and of Man as the measure of all earthly things, the direct outcome of the philosophy of the West; on the other hand, an architecture singularly expressive of the peculiar Hindu mentality and the principle of ultimate re-absorption within the vast immeasurable Cosmos.

CHAPTER 7

HISTORY AND APPLIED SCIENCE

MACAULAY'S severe criticism of Indian culture is well known; in this he discussed the following problems: "The question now before us is simply whether, when it is in our power to teach this language (*i.e.* English), we shall teach languages in which by universal confession there are no books on any subject which deserve to be compared to our own; whether, when we can teach European science, we shall teach systems which by universal confession whenever they differ from those of Europe differ for the worse; and whether, when we can patronize sound philosophy and true history, we shall countenance at the public expense medical doctrines which would disgrace an English farrier, astronomy which would move laughter in girls at an English boarding-school, history abounding with kings thirty feet high and reigns thirty thousand years long, and geography made up of seas of treacle and seas of butter. . . ."[1]

Yet in spite of this damnatory verdict, followed by several generations of Western education in India, these traditions have not ceased to exist; they still live and will continue to live. This is clearly evidenced by the many temples which are being

[1] D. C. Boulger, *Lord William Bentinck*, "Rulers of India," p. 155.

rebuilt according to the ancient styles, as an expression of an ever-powerful tropical imagination, by the agelong social and economic traditions that still defy reform, and by the uncontested authority of the Brahmins, the priestly teachers, especially in the Southern regions of the Malabar coast where extensive swamps frustrate all devices of modern Western technical science, and Brahmanic precepts and doctrines are based even to-day on ancient religious and scientific tradition. It seems as though the apparently primitive concepts that roused Macaulay's criticism were inseparably connected with India's geographical and tropical conditions.

In the previous chapter the foundations of Indian Art were discussed; and with these in mind, it can readily be appreciated that the rich imaginativeness and colour of the Indian languages could spring only from the exuberance and impressiveness of tropical Nature. Inevitably, Western romanticists were spellbound by Indian fairy tales, which convey much of the mysterious charm of Indian jungle life, closely connecting Man, animals and plants with one another. The richness of the lyrical style was also emphasized; in this the manifold voices of Nature resound, and are assigned that rhythm to which the Indian, with his unfailing keenness of eye and ear, is peculiarly alive. Confined by no town walls, but leading a rustic life in daily contact with the perils of a tropical country, he has retained that acuteness of observation which is innate in primitive Man, his body still supple and untrammelled by Western clothing and his limbs enjoying the free play of the child of Nature. Thus a genuine art of the dance could develop and expand in all its subtleness and natural grace; while finally, his plastic Art, as represented by the modellings of the *Gopuras*, shows in its innumerable minute details what can be achieved by the accomplished skill of sensitive hands and a lively imagination.

I shall now turn to Indian History and Science. Here too the course of the development followed by India, in accordance with her own natural conditions, differs essentially from that of the West. For it is inevitable that a people living in a timeless and, in its main characteristics, almost unchanging natural environment could never develop uniqueness, singleness and individualism as their standards of value; hence they never evolved any exact methods of historic research; instead, therefore, of definite historical periods and personalities it is always some "type," marked by exaggerated proportions reflecting the exuberance of Nature, that serves the Hindu as his criterion of value (natural vitality); hence those kingdoms to which Macaulay refers, thirty thousand years old and with rulers thirty feet tall. The only Indian (Kashmirian) historical work which has thus far satisfied Western scholars is the *Rājataranginī*; but its very title shows that it hardly conforms to Western ideas of research, since *Rājataranginī* literally means "Waves of Dynasties." According to its Introduction, then, this chronicle of the Kashmirian kings is intended not to teach facts as a final aim, but to lead the student to the *śānta-rasa* or pacific mood, that is to the mental attitude of an Indian saint totally indifferent towards all earthly happenings. In this unmoved spirit the *Rājataranginī* surveys the oncoming and receding waves of events, neither riding their crests nor plunging into their depths, since according to the Indian conception the history of individuals, families and races is a continuous process of emerging and vanishing, ever subject to the empirical law of continuous change.

Similarly, Indian traditional geography is a cosmography comprising an infinite number of worlds following each other in Space and Time; it envisages continents surrounded by oceans of fertility—Macaulay's seas of sugar, salt and butter. Around these again winds a compact belt of outer mainland alternating with another concentric circle of primeval water, this arrangement being repeated; and this may well serve as a parallel to the Ontology embracing all subordinate systems. Its task is given in its very name, *anu-īkṣikī*, "the survey of all things," its basic concept being the doctrine of transformation and change, while its fundamental assumption is materialistic; nothing comes from nothing, or rather, everything originates from something. With this is associated the *sat-kārya* theory, the postulate that all *kāryas*, all effects, already exist potentially in their cause; a principle supplemented by the *sādharmya*-theory in *Sānkhya-kārikā* 27 and commented upon by Gauḍapāda—that all things are cognate to each other, having descended from the same universal source. Nature is extravagant, yet at the same time economical, substance consumed in one form serving to build up new existents. From this standpoint too has arisen that strange doctrine, expounded in the *Upaniṣads* and adorned with numerous metaphors, of the significance of *anna*, literally "food," or in other words continuously transformed substance and energy, a theory in agreement with modern Western science as exemplified by Mayer's law of the Conservation of Energy.

India's specific attitude towards exact and applied science is likewise impregnated with the same Philosophy of Nature; and it is no mere accident that, even to-day, Indian students in Europe distinguish themselves in certain branches of Science by displaying an inherited talent in its mastery. For they are particularly successful in subjects allied to botany, zoology, medicine and philology

Ancient Indian medical science, again, is concerned with the collective forces running through all living organisms and thus uniting them. Their flow is believed to be increased during certain conjunctions of sun, moon and stars, an idea that has lately been recognized in the West. Herbs and roots are considered particularly helpful in strengthening the human frame, being supposed to be filled with the vital force active in Man himself; in this respect recent Western chlorophyll cures may be cited.

Indian medicine itself is based on an unbroken contact with surrounding Nature, keen observation and a deep knowledge of plant life making the Hindu a strikingly successful pharmacologist; and the *Kavirāj*, with his stock of roots and herbs, is even to-day more patronized than the Western dispensary.

Another characteristic of the Hindu mind derived from its general outlook is a special interest in biology, which appears to influence even a subject so remote as Ethics.[1] The primitive and highly sensitive Indian of early times accurately observed the activities and humours of the body, respiration, the circulation of the blood, the production of gall and other secretions. Indian medical science has, in fact, anticipated the current theories of constitutional types, as dependent on the varying proportions and relative predominance of the glandular products, in its *cakra*- and *padma*-doctrines of the *Tantra Texts*, derived from early *Yoga*-precepts.[2] In the same way, the knowledge of the influence of carriage and posture on physical, and thus on psychical, well-being has been since the earliest times the common property of all Indians with or without special training.[3] Many recent discoveries

[1] *Cf.* Chapter 4.

[2] The constitutional human types are recognized too in the animal kingdom; *cf.* the preceding chapter. A unique section of the Tanjore library contains illustrations and texts on the psycho-biology of horses, elephants, etc., a most valuable contribution to the science of animal-breeding.

[3] For further details *cf. Journ. Roy. Asiat. Soc.*, 1937, pp. 355 ff.

in natural science, such as that of the existence of a plant life-cycle and of pulsation in plants as well as in animals, are the result of the presupposition that all living organisms must share an essentially common structure. The world-famous scientist, Jagadish Chandra Bose, acknowledges his indebtedness for his own remarkable discoveries in plant physiology to the ancient *Upaniṣads*: "The juice of plants is blood, the plants themselves are manifestations of this all-pervading vital unity which my ancestors have propagated three thousand years ago on the banks of the Ganges";[1] and as an expression of this conviction I observed, in Bose's most up-to-date laboratories in Calcutta, symbolic scenes from ancient epics painted on the walls.

But the Hindu long ago developed yet another science: his life, as has already been remarked in the discussion of the foundations of Theology, depends to a marked degree on atmospheric conditions, and to this day he is guided by laws prescribed by the positions of sun and moon. The stars shine brilliantly in the cloudless tropic sky; the strain of a torrid day is followed by the agreeable coolness of night, unless the heat continues to be so oppressive as to prevent sleep, and for many hours the Indian sits and contemplates the starlit sky, thereby acquiring a special facility for astronomical research. It must be admitted, however, that his belief in the favourable or adverse powers of atmospheric conditions, though

[1] Bose, *Atlantis*, 1929, p. 177.

certainly based on exact observation, sometimes converts astronomy into magical astrology.

At this stage in my exposition a glance at the progress of Science in the West will yield a better understanding of its development in India. No sooner had the anthropological period begun in ancient Greece than primitive observation became influenced by the postulate of a logical-aesthetic order of Nature. Receptive and practical contemplation, therefore, was never characteristic of Western astronomy; it was always the regular order observed in the constellations and their periodical return that appealed to the systematic Greek mind; and thus the regulating and regulated order of the celestial orbs was venerated as reflecting the harmony of a divine personality.

Research in other branches of Science is equally closely connected with the natural conditions of Indian life. The monsoon winds and the rains, occurring as they do seasonally, have given a marked impulse to meteorological and climatological studies, while agricultural science is still more involved. For though well over 80 per cent of the population still lead a rustic life in spite of the attempted industrialization imported from the West, the lucrative cultivation of the soil is hardly possible. Some orthodox sects indeed, such as the Jains, owing to their strict observation of the rules of *Ahiṁsā*, prohibit all ploughing and tilling in order not to violate the sacredness of animal life. Still greater difficulties are presented by the problem of mechanized agriculture, since ancient law threatens with caste degradation, or even with capital punishment, the making and use of *Yantras*, *i.e.* machines, because of their interference with the course and rhythm of Nature. Still further, owing to the hostile attitude of the orthodox Indian mind towards the aims of Western economics, which tend to increase rather than diminish human requirements, Occidental economics could never take root in the soil of traditional India.

Indian religion, however, while unquestionably restricting the growth of certain branches of Science, has afforded a powerful impetus to others. Thus the sacrificial altar of ancient *Brāhmaṇa*-times was built according to carefully calculated plans, because every mistake, however small, in adjusting the parts was bound to be magnified owing to its effect on the Macrocosm, and so to assume the proportions of a most serious breach of cosmic laws. I believe that from this source sprang the mathematical sciences, which originated, as it were, from the magical and religious demands of ancient India. Thus Indian geometry and arithmetic have flourished ever since the times when the sacrificial *Texts* of the *Brāhmaṇas* were first composed; and it is equally noteworthy that in India the so-called Pythagorean theorem was not enunciated as an abstract conclusion, but was discovered independently merely through practical experiments in laying out the sacrificial altar. At all stages of the development of thought mathematical symbols have had more than purely mathematical significance. Geometrical symbols are equivalent to the concrete personal expression of the unapproachable Divine, involved triangles, for instance, being used as means of meditation and concentration, like the image of a Deity, as with the *Yantras* of the *Tantra*-systems.[1] Indian arithmetic similarly has its own special complexion, the concept of zero being due not to abstract mathematial deduction, but to empirical observations of polarity in Nature and their application to Ontology and Metaphysics: zero then implying no definite size, or the non-dimensional and the all-dimensional. Accordingly the mathematicians (*e.g.* Bhāskarācārya) identify *Śūnya* (zero) with *Nirvāṇa*.[2]

It is, then, extremely interesting to observe how India has contributed to modern Western mathematics while clinging closely to her own traditional trend of thought. The great Indian mathematician, who recently gave so marked a stimulus to Oxford and Cambridge studies, was Ramanujan, who came to Europe with a system of his own. Not only did he remain an orthodox Hindu, even during his stay in England, in his strict observation of caste rules, but also in his special outlook on mathematics. For he was interested not in abstract mathematical deduction but in solving concrete problems, all his researches being typically Indian. Utilizing so-called "natural" ciphers and their combinations, he began

[1] *Cf.* Chapter 6, "Aesthetics."
[2] *Cf.* Chapter 5, "Logic."

with concrete problems which, as has previously been emphasized with respect to Logic, only in their final consequences lead to the abstract, and continued to argue inductively while he investigated all possible combinations of these "natural" numbers. He was deeply interested, too, in the so-called "empiric" numbers, or "concrete" ciphers; from his empirical and concrete Indian standpoint he refused to recognize abridgments which combine single numbers in any abstract unity, as had already been attempted in the West by the early Greek mathematicians. Ramanujan succeeded, nonetheless, in his most complicated calculations, whether owing to a typically Indian intuitive anticipation, or by painstaking calculations and humble devotion to his heavy task, aided throughout by an inherited sense of duty (caste!). In the very statement of his problems, in fact, he was obviously following a tendency which, as was pointed out in the previous chapter, is inherent in all Indian Art: for it was not the novelty of a problem, but its repetitive treatment and minute variation, that appealed to this great Indian mathematician.

The most important branch of Science, however, to be derived from India's *Weltanschauung* is philology; and not until the ancient Indian treatises on linguistics became known in the West could the new foundations of scientific grammar be established there. Franz Bopp, the founder of modern comparative philology, based his own work on Indian models, while it was from India that the subtle laws of phonetics and grammatical analysis came to the kindred European languages. The Hindu dissects each word-organism into its living constituents (hence the Sanskrit term for "Grammar," *Vy-ā-karaṇa*, *i.e.* analysis!), thus leading to a fertile analysis of word compounds, even in proper names, so that each constituent can be replaced by some synonym. From this embarrassing interchangeability of words, undeniably, difficulties may arise for the Western interpreter, as when he finds for one and the same town the two names *Puṣpa-pura* and *Kusuma-pura*, but fails to recognize that both have the same meaning—"flower-town." A synonym may be inserted in proper names also, these being always key-words possessing vivid functional meaning, never dead abstract nouns. Thus, for instance, the Western investigator will vainly ask whether the name of the founder of the atomic theory in the *Vaiśeṣika* system was Kaṇāda, Kaṇabhuj, Kaṇabhakṣa or Kaṇabhakṣana; for these all mean exactly the same, "atom-eater" or "atom-enjoyer," which again is probably no accidental individual name but a functional *ad hoc* appellation, derived from his very theory.

From a methodological point of view another form of typically Indian grammatical analysis is of far-reaching importance. In Sanskrit, the dynamic stem of the verbal root is clearly recognizable between prefix and suffix in all its derivations, to which it serves as a key. This facilitates an unequalled simplification of linguistic research, since one single root renders intelligible the whole of its derivatives and affords valuable insight into the organic development of language. The phonetic subtlety, again, is the direct result of the Indian's proximity to Nature, of the unimpaired keenness of his sense-organs and his magical susceptibility to impressions in general.

Instruction by Indian scholars was always mainly oral, and even to-day the true *Pandit* teaches without books; learning and understanding therefore depend above all on sharp attention and hearing. The colour of the vowels (*varṇa*), the articulation of the sonants, whether hard or soft, and their mutual combinations, have gradually developed into an accurate phonetic system; while in addition to the rational meaning of a term, the Indian also takes into consideration the purely non-rational suggestive effect of the sound or rhythm itself. Just as a relationship is believed to exist between all the constituents of the Cosmos, so a psychological relationship is established between all words of similar sound; and the sensitive ear of the child of Nature distinguishes the characteristic animal modes of expression, and consequently recognizes in this way every living creature. Onomatopoeia is thus more finely developed in Sanskrit than in any Western language, and Western linguists may, in this as in other respects, gain much from the study of Indian philology.

A few words, in conclusion, on Indian and Western

physics. The general Indian view rests on two fundamental principles: in the first place there is an intense study of physical phenomena in themselves, involving concrete observation that prevents the student escaping too quickly into the abstract deductions of systematizing theory; Hindus are therefore past masters in experiment and patient observation of minute details. Secondly, the Indian has never indulged, at least till very recent times, in that artificial dissection of the subject matter adopted by European science ever since Aristotle laid down its foundations. Among the latest holders of the Nobel Prize in physics, as is well known, is Raman, the discoverer of the "Raman effect"; and the two tendencies, immanent in all Indian thought, have very materially contributed to his success, the "Raman effect" being based on the postulate that molecular theory cannot be divorced from the neighbouring domain of chemistry. Still further, it is usually only after a large number of experiments has been meticulously performed that any important generalization is discovered, and in this vital respect India's traditional outlook is at one with the most recent tendency in Western Science. But in my final chapter a fuller discussion will be undertaken of these problems, arising from the apparent approximation of Western anthropological speculation to the strictly consistent cosmic views of the East.

In reply to Macaulay's drastic criticisms, then, I may conclude with a simile taken from the field of botany. Nature, we fully realize, admits a vast range of possibilities; and from many parts of a plant-system leaves and blossoms may branch off. Now it is the vitality and creative energy of these sideshoots that determine the value of the system, not the height of the stem from which they have sprung. It may be, therefore, that the base of India's culture is at a much lower level than that of Western civilizations, which have doubtless grown to a more imposing height. Nevertheless this by no means involves any comparative deficiency in creative power in India. On the contrary: it may well be that, just because the stem of India's culture has clung so firmly to the level of earth, it has preserved to a greater degree than Occidental systems its unbroken consistency and retained the hardy vitality of a creeper that entwines the gigantic trees in the virgin forest.

CHAPTER 8

THE APPARENT *RAPPROCHEMENT* BETWEEN WEST AND EAST

In the previous chapter I treated India's applied sciences as being the consistent outcome of her general anthropo-geographical view. Certainly some of her achievements accidentally fitted into some Western developments, and thus formed valuable contributions to Western science in spite of having been conceived from an essentially different angle. I shall now approach my subject from the opposite direction and glance at those Occidental developments wherein some individuals, remote from the main line of thought, attempted to follow paths off the beaten track that seemed to lead to the consistent cosmic views of India: men who spent their lives in monasteries or lonely rectories in the North, meditating on the stillness of Nature as contrasted with an outside world bent on temporal pleasure and resounding with the clamour of earthly struggles. To begin with: St. Francis of Assisi who, in the solitude of a hillside monastery in Italy's sunlit woods, listened to the sweet song of the birds; his brethren who, in the remoteness of sombre Spanish monasteries, found mystical expression for their fervent love of God and, for His sake, of all His creatures. But these lonely mystics are merely transient phenomena in the West, and have never very deeply influenced a world absorbed in political strife, but have only accentuated their own personal aloofness from the masses of mankind. Certainly the Franciscan brotherhood tried to impress wider circles by its charity and its ideals of poverty and humility; yet this does not alter the fact that the recluse and his secular followers were, while fighting against a selfish world blinded by passion, still children of the Western temperate zone with its pleasant climatic conditions. Even in their religious convictions, moreover, they were bound to obey their superiors; and though freed from political claims, they considered themselves as subject to the higher religious authorities and to their heavenly Master. Love of animals and plants, therefore, was but another mode of expressing their humble attitude towards God and His creatures. We are not concerned here, however, with the question whether these instances constitute an actual *rapprochement* to Indian ideas or not, since hermits and their few followers were never regarded as adequate representatives of the West.

More important and worthier of comparison with India's primitive basis appear those recent outbreaks which, after two and a half millennia of the uncontested reign of anthropological ideas, flame up here and there from the depths of the emotional Western soul alike in religion and politics, in natural science and art, as a fully conscious reaction against Western rationalism and individualism. These compel us to ask whether there has been any true *rapprochement* between Western and Eastern thought. For here we are at last confronted with a general movement that seems to have seized all Western civilization, and the Sophist's static doctrine of "Man as the measure of all things" appears to be impugned. Are we to think that this recent doubt as to the validity of all established Western categories implies the acknowledgment that the primitive cosmic base of speculation had been discarded too early by the Sophists, before, indeed, all the fruits which this fertile soil might have yielded had been gathered? Are we now reverting to those older foundations, and recognizing that the poorer soil of anthropological thought is well-nigh exhausted? Let us inquire, then, whether the West, in its search for new bases, is about to reoccupy the very ground which Eastern culture has never abandoned. A further question: Can the West, in spite of its recent change of doctrine, still claim to raise the East to what is called the "higher level" of Occidental culture as, for instance, was openly stated at the last International Conference on Ethnology during the discussion of the treatment of native races? Or is there, owing to the very fact of the current and apparently fundamental changes in the West, a better prospect of mutual collaboration on terms of equality between East and West? Must we continue to accept Kipling's familiar dictum—"East is East, and West is West, and never the twain shall meet"? Or may we modify it thus—"East is East and West will become East, and therefore they will meet"? Or rather—"East is East and West remains West, even in this apparent *rapprochement*, and so they may meet after all in mutual collaboration and for their reciprocal enrichment"?

I venture on a brief scrutiny of this important Occidental development. In the first place, Science has changed many of its hitherto most fundamental categories; Space and Time have both become relative concepts instead of absolute. It is now possible, still further, to reach the remotest parts of the world in a comparatively short time, telegraph, telephone and radio affording extremely rapid communication. Thus modern Science has discovered methods leading to a new type of transcendentalism; mankind is transgressing spatial limits both by invading the stratosphere and by telescopically observing processes occurring in remote sidereal systems.

Modern machines, to continue, are constantly accelerating production; and thus Time is no longer an absolute category. Man's labour, too, has ceased to afford him spiritual support; he is never alone with tasks endeared to him by slow and toilsome progress, sometimes extending over many years or even a lifetime; in fact, the connection between Man and his work has been relaxed by mass-production to the last possible degree. Thus the personal contact, enjoying an almost religious intimacy, between work and worker has been destroyed, the "moving belt" permitting only an impersonal contact with thousands of unfinished parts of the whole; and the craftsman's devotion to quality has been replaced by considerations of mere quantity.

Just as the categories of Time, Space and Quality have been expanded by Western Science, so the dimensional category too has lost all fixed significance; skyscrapers equal towns in size and huge liners are gigantic hotels. On the other hand, extreme minuteness has become a criterion of visible magnitudes; the "splitting of the atom" facilitates the approximation to the smallest entities. Spatial, temporal and dimensional relativity dethroning the hitherto unquestioned order of values, and thus approaching the primitive confusion between quantity and quality, is the inevitable outcome of modern invention and discovery.

The relativity of all Man's hitherto fixed categories has also perturbed the Western standard of his status in the Cosmos. On the one hand, the principle of δεινὸς ἀνήρ (master and measure of all things) has now gained the sanction provided by all his marvellous achievements, even while it is this very predominance that has been shaken by Man's own discoveries. Irony of Fate! The heliocentric theory has for several centuries held undisputed sway; Man and his world are no longer singled out from other cosmic systems; their centre of gravity has been displaced; Man himself is but one of the many possible cosmic beings of countless other galaxies.

How then can the West, faced with these universally accepted conclusions, adhere to its postulate that the path of Western culture is the only possible one? Are not these discoveries and their logical consequences reviving afresh the ancient cosmic outlook of the pre-Sophist world, which coincides so closely with that of India?

Nevertheless the Indian *Weltanschauung* is itself no outcome of Western scientific research. That Cosmos is not the transcendental Universe of innumerable star-systems, but rather a terrestial cosmos based on unbroken contact with all other fellow-beings on or around the earth alone. It is true that modern Biology and Palaeontology also acknowledge, in one way, this limited cosmos, since they have ascertained the connecting links between Man and other forms of life, both animal and plant. Nonetheless do they employ these data to support the Western hypotheses of progressive development from lower to higher forms, in this way upholding the doctrine that Man approaches more nearly to perfection than all other creatures. Still further, the connection between humanity and other living species has been relaxed by his old animal servants being replaced almost completely by machines, while many important vegetable ingredients that assist bodily regeneration can now be displaced by chemical synthetic products. Thus the new cosmic sense which is arising in the West leads not to the primitive and visible realm of Nature, but beyond it.

If, however, this holds true of the content of Occidental Science, perhaps its methods are reverting to the primal complexity that preceded the analysis of its subject matter. It may certainly be granted that these systematic subdivisions are no longer maintained as they were originally conceived and enunciated by Aristotle and his ancient and medieval followers. As has been observed in the preceding chapter, each single science depends for its success on contributions from closely affiliated, and even the more remote, branches of knowledge. Further, Mathematics has recently established intimate associations with Philosophy and Logic, the best-known example being probably Russell and Whitehead's *Principia Mathematica*. This new development, however, stands somewhat apart, and is not based on empirical observation as is Indian practical and ontological mathematics; it is, in other words, not the general science of *anu-īkṣikī*, or receptive contemplation of established empirical facts.

It may therefore be asked whether modern Western relativity is at all comparable to the Eastern attitude of mind, with its sensitiveness to all intuition and its reluctance to recognize reasoning as the highest capacity. True, the reliability of reason has even in the West been seriously perturbed by the very results of reasoning. The so-called Laws of Nature, imposed nevertheless by the controlling mind of Man, have become susceptible to a menacing number of important exceptions. But far from despairing of that doubtful instrument, his reasoning mind, Man continues to use it to increase the accuracy and efficiency of his technical methods, overstraining his brain in restless search for still farther-reaching discoveries. Leisure is no longer left for solitude devoted to fruitful meditation and humble expectation of divine intuition; but it was only the quiet of a culture, knowing no time restrictions, that could give birth to India's intuitive vision.

As against all this, the psychological consequences of the recent Western discoveries establishing the relativity of hitherto established categories have led implicitly to a new non-rationality, to a search for refuge in mysticism and emotionalism of all shades. Once more, however, this is not the consistent non-rationalism that India has developed. New religions arise too, striving to prove Oriental ideas by Western arguments, which they cannot evade. Modern religious edifices sufficiently illustrate this, being erected in the sober style of secular buildings with only few religious ornaments and symbols. Nonetheless we may some day witness a new cult in the very centre of Europe: a new type of non-rational religiosity has sprung from a peculiar intermixture of political sentiment with a vague, yet irresistible religious urge; a modern mythology and hero-worship, in fact, have come into existence.

In another direction, Russia affords an extremely interesting example of the genuinely religious veneration of technical progress, her emotions, which formerly found their outlet in the worship of icons and the gorgeous rites of the church, now being spent in fervent devotion to the ideal of a mechanized community. This is really one curious mode of expression of the widespread current emotional reaction, to be found also in other countries, against any integral rationalism. It includes at the same moment the adoration of modern achievement and an intense psychological reaction against this. India, on the other hand, has preserved her innate reluctance to adopt any mechanization which tends to disturb the cosmic balance of power. Although the Hindu may have turned Western inventions to account wherever the geographical conditions of his country permitted this, still he has never allowed them to influence his traditional attitude of mind; and if the orthodox Hindu now uses rail and motor car, this does not imply that he has relinquished his inborn devotion to his ancient religion. Even when the masses pour out of the railway carriages which they employ to shorten the time spent on the long journeys to their most sacred places of pilgrimage, they kneel before the altars of their native gods with the same devout prayers and rites as of yore. And when the orthodox Hindu recognizes some recently discovered force of Nature, such as electricity, this immediately assumes for him the significance of a new deity whom he readily receives into his Pantheon, exactly as in the Middle Ages the strange properties of mercury became an object of veneration. India's Pantheon, indeed, can be increased indefinitely, in accord with her age-old belief in the sacred manifoldness of Nature, which permits no exaltation of one of her manifestations above others.

It may be, then, that some recent psychological Occidental reactions closely approximate to the genuine type of Indian non-rationality, since it is admitted that in modern Western Science, even as applied, the non-rational factors play an increasingly important part.

As has just been indicated, emotion—to which may be added the unbridled will to dominate—has found an adequate outlet in some Western political systems. As with mechanization in Russia, so social and political problems too are approached from an emotional, and indeed almost religious, angle. Fascism and Communism, that is to say, are really new forms of religion. But here again no actual analogy is possible with India's traditional spiritual attitude, since the religio-psychological presuppositions, as well as the programmes, of these Western movements occupy a totally different level. From the psychological point of view, however, real political emotion is wholly incompatible with the traditional Indian indifference towards all temporal matters.[1]

With regard to the programme, in the first place, it is obvious that India's caste differences render any unifying collectivism absolutely impossible. The

[1] *Cf.* Chapter 4.

system rests, primarily, not only on the principle of the division of labour, but also on the undeniable inequalities of faculties and functions. According to the Hindu biological viewpoint, the organism of the State can survive only by setting up insurmountable caste distinctions. It may certainly be true that the idea of division of labour, according to which special functions are assigned to individuals within the community, has lately gained ground in the West too; nonetheless must it be recognized that there is always a political background, whether nationalist or international-socialist, that is quite strange to India.

But is there some similarity between India's biological principles and the modern eugenic doctrines propagated by some political theories? As was observed in the chapter on Ethics, India has a keen sense of sex hygiene, marriage outside the clan (exogamy), but within the caste (endogamy), being prescribed by her laws. The limits separating the castes, however, do not coincide with those erected elsewhere between races. In this important respect the caste regulations are of greater severity, since they prohibit marriage, even within the same race, between members of different castes. Still further, no artificial interference with Nature would on any account be sanctioned by orthodox Indian law, sterilization and abortion being strictly prohibited.

Nor can collectivism play any important rôle in the orthodox society of India, the reason again lying in the inflexible character of the caste system itself, which presents most effective barriers against the formation of any wider units possessing political significance. Modern anti-individualism in no degree corresponds to Hindu traditional non-individualism. Each member of Indian society has his due place and functions assigned to him; each enjoys some measure of importance as representing his *Dharma*, or function, within the community, however insignificant he may be as an individual. The problems of individuality, it should be remembered, have never yet been raised in orthodox India; there is not, therefore, and there never has been, any necessity for the Hindu to restrain individual ambition or check individual pride, simply because he is genuinely possessed of neither.

As for the economic ideals of anti-capitalistic groups, once more the fundamental difference between traditional India and a constantly changing West must be emphasized. All Occidental politico-economic creeds tend in practice to advance the means and methods of production, although this tendency may not always be theoretically implied. This however is never the view of orthodox India, which on the contrary stresses the antithetic ideal of diminishing human requirements. Indifference towards capitalism, therefore, not antagonism, would be the natural Hindu attitude.

The Indian's characteristic unconcern as to his own transient personality, again, and his unconditional obedience to the functions, duties and rights of castes may lead both to worldly activity and to inactive meditation, according to the widely different requirements of the Hindu periods of life.[1] Thus the *Bhagavadgītā* has recently been interpreted in different political quarters as the "Song in praise of fighting"; but it is quite inadmissible to draw any parallel between this ancient Indian extolling of the warrior's duty in combat, and any political dogma of the West, since the *Bhagavadgītā* explicitly recognizes contest only as a neutral obligation free from emotional personal concern. Moreover, the warrior's duty is merely a part of the general system of *Dharmas* connecting all beings in the Universe; and it is from this mutual relationship that the Indian idea of *Ahiṁsā*, as was remarked in the chapter on Ethics, deduces its fundamental precept of tolerance and acknowledgment of all other duties and rights. Here too, then, analogies with India would be quite fruitless.

A brief glance at the tendencies operating in contemporary European music, painting, plastic art and architecture will suffice to prove that not one of these lends itself to comparison with the East. We shall find, in fact, that the fundamental contrasts between the cultures of East and West are nowhere so strikingly evident as in the sphere of Art.

As to music in the first place, whether old or new, any analogy between Western "art" and Eastern "sound" is excluded for quite obvious

[1] *Cf*. Chapter 4.

reasons; and except that both use the medium of sound they have nothing whatever in common. "Exotic," but not necessarily Oriental, elements absorbed into Western music will certainly modify, or even radically change, its laws, but they will not touch what is its very essence—emotion as the outcome of mental unrest, of doubt or struggle, of personal joy and despair. All this, however, is conspicuously absent in the traditional music of the East, characterized by its monotony achieved by the endless repetition of short melodious phrases, though these by no means altogether preclude subtle variations which can neither be understood nor fully appreciated by the Western musical sense. But the highly emotional significance of wide intervals, dynamic variety and distinct rhythm will ever be strange to the peace of Eastern melody, in which there is not the faintest echo of Western struggle and unrest of mind.

In modern Western painting, again, the current tendency is to convey an impression of cosmic manifoldness not by any exuberance of detail but, on the contrary, by merging line and colour and thus achieving the effect of unity.

In Western graphic and plastic art the artist, now as ever, does not surrender to the bewildering multiplicity of the cosmic phenomena around him; his attitude towards these, unlike that of the Hindu, is dominating, or in other terms he simplifies and arranges them according to his own regulative personality. Dürer's dictum, therefore, is still valid for the West: "Art is hidden in Nature; snatch it from her grasp and it is yours."[1]

Similarly in modern Western architecture a non-sensuous rationalism has led to the development of a style which, in all its simplicity and soberness, presents the completest possible contrast to India's exuberant *baroque* with its interweaving of definite cosmic forms.

Summing up, then, in the West two strangely contradictory attempts to overcome the moral, political and economic dilemma of the present day predominate: on the one hand, an exaggerated rationalism; on the other, an equally exaggerated and forced emotionalism assuming the guise of political, religious, scientific and artistic movements. Both alike, however, are inevitable developments, and perhaps the final consequences, of the primal anthropological idea, even though they may also be reactions from this. But in no event will the changeable West ever return to an undisturbed harmony with any earthly cosmos. For India's collectivism and non-individualism, her relativity of values and sense of infinity, are all naturally antipathetic to the spasmodic actions and reactions of the West. Any apparent *rapprochement*, therefore, really removes both types of culture further apart, and increasingly

[1] *Die Kunst steckt in der Natur; wer sie heraus kann reissen, der hat sie* (*cf.* Lange-Fuhse, *Dürer's schriftlicher Nachlass*, pp. 226 and 363).

reveals their inherently different tendencies. In the West the antitheses are never harmonized, but simply indicate painful attempts to terminate transient struggles. The exaggeration of both mechanical production and emotional stresses constitutes a contrast which is not recognized by Nature herself.

We seem driven to conclude, therefore, that the divergent lines of West and East belong to wholly different planes, so that even if they sometimes appear to converge, still they will never meet.

EPILOGUE

THE object of my comparative Study is of course not simply to indicate certain traits in the cultural systems of East and West which may occasionally and, as it were, accidentally resemble each other in one way or the other. Rather have I striven to stress the necessity for moving on two different planes simultaneously, thus widening our view and at the same moment approaching more closely the *Śānta-rasa* in the historical sense of the *Rājataranginī*, surveying, that is to say, the oncoming and receding waves of events with unmoved spirit. Thus the troubles of the day attain their due relativity.[1]

There should, however, be also a positive methodical gain as to the range of possibilities of the human mind. For the Anthropological, and the Cosmic, speculative tendencies may be compared to huge cell nuclei round which cellular protoplasm gathers concentrically, gradually increasing both in density and in volume; and although the peripheral regions may lack compactness, still they remain centred on their respective nuclei. Pursuing this metaphor, there is no reason whatever to assume that these two *quasi*-biological systems, the Anthropological and the Cosmic, are the only possible centres which the human mind has hitherto been able, or will be able in future, to develop productively and consistently.

[1] *Cf.* Chapter 7.

INDEX OF PROBLEMS TREATED

(*A*)

PROBLEMS ANSWERED DIFFERENTLY BY EAST AND WEST

(*C*)

PHILOLOGICAL-PHILOSOPHICAL SYNOPSIS OF TERMS

PAGES

Anu-īkṣikī, lit. look along (*anu*). Hence: philosophy as investigation and reflection . 27; and *passim*

Avidyā, lit. non-knowledge = Māyā, i.e. discrimination of isolated objects . . . . . 92 ff.

Bhatki, lit. participation. In theology: union of devotee and object of devotion . . . 35 ff.; 73 f.

Darśana (*dṛṣṭi*), lit. a seeing. In religious psychology: vision; in epistemology: knowledge; general term: system 28

Dharma, lit. fixed position. Legal term: a statute; in ethics: duty, right; in ontology: law of Nature; in Buddhism: precepts of Buddha; in later Buddhist epistemology: the phenomena as data . . . . 68 ff.; 78; 142

Karma, lit. action. In theory of perception: category of motion; in grammatical science: direct object (accusative case); in ethics: action and reaction . . . . . 35; 42; 47 f.; 60 f.; 70 f.

Māyā, lit. a measuring. In philosophy: all measurable (i.e. all empirical) objects. In Buddhism and Vedānta esp. illustion, as contrasted with transcendental reality . . . 49 ff., esp. 53; 94 f.

PAGES

Nirvāna, lit. blown off. In ontology: dispersion of all definite shape; in logic: (dis)solution of all definition; in psychology: (dis)solution of all individual desire . . . . . 49; 53 f.

Rṭa, lit. a going. In ontology: functional immanent order of the cosmic phenomena; in theology: divine law; in epistemology: truth . 34 f.; 74

Sat, lit. being (pres. part. of to be). In ontology: existent; in ethics: good; in epistemology: true (*cf.* satya) 56; 75; 82

Upādhi, lit. to place near, to put upon. In logic and theology: wrong attribution, wrong discrimination 80

Yantra, lit. causing to go or to restrain (polarity of meaning!). General: any instrument, implement, or machine; hence in ethics: interference with the course of Nature . . . . 82; 124 f.

Yoga, lit. union. In astronomy: a conjunction of stars; in arithmetics: addition; in grammatical science: etymological association; in Yoga System: concentration of body and mind . 52; 96; 121 f.

GEORGE ALLEN & UNWIN LTD
London: 40 Museum Street, W.C.1
Leipzig: (F. Volckmar) Hospitalstr. 10
Cape Town: 73 St. George's Street
Toronto: 91 Wellington Street, West
Bombay: 15 Graham Road, Ballard Estate
Wellington, N.Z.: 8 Kings Crescent, Lower Hutt
Sydney, N.S.W.: Australia House, Wynyard Square